The International Library of Sociology

APPRENTICESHIP

I0462076

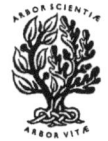

Founded by KARL MANNHEIM

THE SOCIOLOGY OF
WORK AND ORGANIZATION
In 18 Volumes

APPRENTICESHIP

An Enquiry into its Adequacy
under Modern Conditions

by
KATE LIEPMANN

Foreword by
H. D. DICKINSON

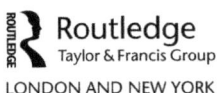
Routledge
Taylor & Francis Group
LONDON AND NEW YORK

First published in 1960 by
Routledge

Reprinted in 1998 by
Routledge
2 Park Square, Milton Park, Abingdon, Oxon, OX14 4RN
711 Third Avenue, New York, NY 10017

Transferred to Digital Printing 2007

Routledge is an imprint of the Taylor & Francis Group

First issued in paperback 2013

British Library Cataloguing in Publication Data
A CIP catalogue record for this book
is available from the British Library

Apprenticeship
ISBN13: 978-0-415-17673-6 (hardback)
ISBN13: 978-0-415-86847-1 (paperback)

The Sociology of Work and Organization: 18 Volumes
ISBN 0-415-17829-0
The International Library of Sociology: 274 Volumes
ISBN 0-415-17838-X

ISBN 0-415-17838-X

Publisher's Note
The publisher has gone to great lengths to ensure the quality of this reprint
but points out that some imperfections in the original may be apparent

CONTENTS

ABBREVIATIONS

A.E.U.	Amalgamated Engineering Union
A.M.I.Mech.E.	Associate Member, Institution of Mechanical Engineers
A.T.I.	Association of Technical Institutions, i.e. technical colleges
B.A.C.	Bristol Aeroplane Company Ltd.
B.A.T.C.	Building Apprenticeship and Training Council
B.E.M.A.	Bristol Engineering Manufacturers Association
C. & G.	City and Guilds of London Institute
C.J.E.E., C.Y.E.E.	Central Youth (originally, Juvenile) Employment Executive
D.C.S.	Day Continuation School
E.T.U.	Electrical Trades Union
F.E.	Further Education
G.C.E.	General Certificate of Education—(O) : ordinary, (A) : advanced level
H.N.C.	Higher National Certificate
L.E.A.	Local Education Authority
O.N.C.	Ordinary National Certificate
S.1	First year of Senior Course leading to O.N.C. Examination
T.A.	Typographical Association
Y.E.O.	Youth Employment Officer
Y.E.S.	Youth Employment Service

FOREWORD

By H. D. Dickinson

Professor of Economics, University of Bristol

THIS study of Apprenticeship was written by my colleague, Dr. Kate Liepmann, with the help of a grant made available by the Ministry of Labour and National Service under the Conditional Aid scheme for the use of Counterpart Funds derived from United States Economic Aid.

It gives me great pleasure to write a foreword to this book, because I believe it to be a thoroughly sound and worth-while piece of research. I have been in constant communication with Dr. Liepmann during the progress of the work and have seen it gradually take shape and come to completion. With the general tenor of the work and with its main conclusions I am in full agreement.

I would emphasise the fact that not all the evidence upon which its conclusions rest can be given, because of the fog of secretiveness and confidentiality that hangs round nearly all investigations into business and trade-union life in Britain. Many of Dr. Liepmann's statements that appear to rest on somewhat slender evidence are, in fact, much more firmly based than they seem.

A study like this touches at its periphery upon so many other fields of knowledge that it was impracticable to pursue all the possible connections of the subject. General economic theory, the theory of collective bargaining, industrial psychology, work-study, social anthropology—upon all these disciplines a study of Apprenticeship could impinge, and all these could throw additional light upon the central subject. But the author judged—and I agreed with her—that it was better to resist these temptations to further development of the thesis, in order to keep the book short and compact.

H.D.D.

vii

PREFACE

In recent years, Apprenticeship has become a matter of general concern. Evidence of this can be seen in the appointment, in 1956, of the Carr Committee and in the interest aroused by the Committee's Report *Training for Skill—Recruitment and Training of Young Workers in Industry* (1958). The Carr Report and the discussion centred on it not only show the importance of the subject but also indicate the need for independent and detailed research in this field. Several recent books have greatly increased our knowledge of apprenticeship conditions ; but the problems involved are so many-sided and complex that an additional study of the apprenticeship system needs no apology.

Because certain features of apprenticeship are changing continuously and rapidly, it is inevitable that in a study of this kind some of the facts should be out of date by the time of publication. However, since the fundamental factors do not change so quickly, the general conclusions of the investigation should retain their validity.

In the fieldwork on which this book is based I was assisted by two investigation officers : Mr. A. Angles, B.Com. (from January to March 1955) and Mrs. Sonya Miles (from June 1955 to December 1956). Mrs. Miles did most of the interview work ; without her insight and efficient interviewing the conclusions would have rested on much weaker foundations. By her contribution in this and in other ways, she has no small share in the preparation of this study.

I should like to express my sincere thanks for the grant made available by the Ministry of Labour under the Conditional Aid scheme and also for a grant towards the cost of publication from the University of Bristol.

I am grateful to the firms who provided information by completing a questionnaire and to the managers, training officers, and employees of all ranks who answered questions in personal interviews.

PREFACE

I greatly profited by discussions with secretaries of employers' associations and of trade unions, with heads and staffs of technical colleges and of secondary schools, and with Youth Employment Officers. I was able to draw on the knowledge and experience of many Ministry of Labour officials and wish to record my appreciation of their co-operative attitude to this enquiry.

I am greatly indebted to the heads of the Department of Economics, Professor H. D. Dickinson and Professor R. C. Tress, and to my colleagues B. D. Giles and N. Robertson, who read parts of the manuscript and made valuable suggestions. I am especially beholden to Professor Dickinson, whose advice, criticism, and generosity supported me in all stages of the work.

The staff of the University Library, in particular that of the Library of the Institute of Education, have put me into their debt by help on many occasions.

K.L.

Department of Economics,
University of Bristol.
August, 1959.

I

INTRODUCTION

THE concept of apprenticeship is characterised by the duality of its nature: the apprentice is both learning and earning, the employer is both training him and paying him for productive work. Apprenticeship thus forms part of the system of education and part of the economic system, and the adequacy of apprenticeship turns largely upon its success in harmonizing the interests of education and of production.

A third important factor, though not inherent in the concept, is the trade-union attitude to apprenticeship. The apprentice is the future craftsman, as distinct from the semi-skilled worker and the labourer; hence apprenticeship is greatly affected by the craftsmen's concern with their status, with differential wages, and with demarcation rules.

The stage on which apprenticeship has been set for hundreds of years is the individual firm; it is the employer who pays the apprentice, puts him to work and causes him to acquire the practical knowledge of his trade. Technical education, which is provided in the main by Local Education Authorities, is a comparatively recent development; it is not a precondition of apprenticeship.

The apprentice is a member of the labour force; the conditions of his employment are laid down in general National Agreements between trade unions and employers' associations.

Most features of apprenticeship have roots deep in the past. By contrast, in the past few decades there have been revolutionary technical, economical and social changes with a bearing on industry; and the educational system is being transformed. Hence the question arises of how adequately apprenticeship is adapted to *modern* conditions.

Rapid change will, no doubt, continue, especially under the impact of automation; the training of apprentices is therefore adequate only if it makes them adaptable to future changes, both in their own interest and for the sake of the flexibility of the country's economic structure.

The industries to be investigated—Engineering, Printing and the Trowel Trades (Building)—were selected with a view to their local importance and to their significant differences as to apprenticeship conditions, degree of mechanisation, 'de-skilling' and attractiveness to boys. Boot and Shoe Manufacture, an industry without apprenticeship, has been included for comparison.

Each of the industries has distinctive features in the field of apprenticeship and training; both these and the features which they have in common make for deeper understanding of the general issues involved.

(a) Engineering commands the greatest interest. On the one hand, craftsmanship and apprenticeship in Engineering are influenced by mechanisation in the same way as in other industries: ever-increasing use of machines and instruments leads to the de-skilling of traditional trades. But, on the other hand, engineering is the very maker of the machines, and therefore an industry growing strongly both in numbers employed and in the skill required by part of its labour force. A differentiation of apprenticeship grades is emerging, allowing for the various levels of skill required in the industry.

(b) Printing: apprenticeship is conducted on traditional lines, and the craft unions' restrictionist influence is very marked; but there are indications that the craftsman's position is beginning to be challenged in several ways.

(c) Building (Bricklayers and Plasterers): the trowel trades are interesting because of continual lack of co-ordination between the supply of, and the demand for, apprentices; strong fluctuations of building activity (cyclical and through changes in Government policy); unrealistic stipulations regarding technical education; prima-facie evidence of over-training, especially in the case of plasterers; organisation of both employers and workers is weak.

INTRODUCTION

(d) Boot and Shoe Manufacture: there are no apprentices, but only learners (expecting to become operatives) on the one hand, and on the other, design and technology students. However, operatives have not just to feed the machines but to manipulate them skilfully; (The Registrar General classifies cutters, clickers, etc., as 'Skilled Workers'). Based on scientific work study, the Boot and Shoe industry has been developing very detailed schemes for teaching operatives their jobs within a short time. An interesting development is the recent adoption of an apprenticeship scheme for prospective foremen only; (this scheme has not yet been introduced in the South-West Region, however).

Geographically, the study is based on the Bristol district and on a rural area in North Somerset; for reasons given in the subsequent section on the source material, the Chippenham (Wiltshire) works of the Westinghouse Brake and Signal Co. Ltd. has been included. The findings of the enquiry will be partly peculiar to the survey area, but partly they will be representative of the relevant state of affairs in the country as a whole.

As with space, so with time: an investigation made in the years 1954 to 1956 will show up some permanent conditions and long-term trends, but also some merely temporary circumstances.

Conditions have changed considerably during the time taken by the enquiry, particularly in the field of technical education. To mention only one important local change over the past few years, the various departments of the Bristol College of Technology have been moved one by one from out-dated, narrow buildings to spacious premises with up-to-date equipment.

As to the future, of one important change it can be foreseen not only that it will happen but also when it will happen, namely the impending reversion from the present shortage of juvenile workers to a 'bulge' of school leavers. Other expected developments, such as automation, are less accurately predictable, but enough is known[1] of the implications of automation for employment to make it urgently necessary to examine the adequacy of the apprenticeship system in view of these problems.

[1] see, e.g., D.S.I.R., *Automation* (1956).

3

INTRODUCTION

The Source Material

Information has been collected from the following sources: (a) regional and local offices of the Government Departments concerned with apprenticeship, particularly the Ministry of Labour and National Service; (b) Local Education Authorities; (c) employers' associations and trade unions; (d) managers and employees at all levels in a number of firms; (e) miscellaneous meetings and personal contacts.

(a) In the Regional Office of the Ministry of Labour, many sections have been consulted, mainly in the Youth Employment Branch and in the National Service Department; also the Statistics and Research section. Locally, managers of employment exchanges and Youth Employment Officers gave us information, and so did the officials of a Government Training Centre.

Relevant material belonging to the S.W. Regional Board of Industry was put at our disposal. We have consulted with the Bristol and Bath Local Productivity Association, and with the Regional Council for Further Education for the South West.

(b) Local Education Authorities furnished information through a variety of offices and committees, colleges and schools. In Bristol, these include the Youth Employment Office and Committee, the Further Education Office; The College of Technology, the College of Commerce, the Day Continuation School; heads of secondary grammar, technical and modern schools; the Youth Officer and youth leaders. In Somerset we had contact with the county's Further Education Officer and with the Technical Institute, Street; in Gloucestershire, with the Kingswood College of Boot and Shoe Manufacture; in Wiltshire with the Technical College, Chippenham. We also met several of H.M. Inspectors of Schools.

(c) The following employers' associations provided information: the Engineering and Allied Employers' West of England Association, also its Department of Work Study; the Bristol Engineering Manufacturers' Association (B.E.M.A.);

4

the Bristol Master Printers and Allied Trades Association; the South Western Federation of Building Trades Employers and its Bristol branch; the Federation of Master Builders, South-west Region; the Bristol and the Kingswood Boot Manufacturers' Associations.

Our trade-union informants include the Bristol Trades Council; the A.E.U. at district, branch and factory level; the Association of Engineering and Shipbuilding Draughtsmen; the various printing craft unions and also non-craft unions in the industry; the trowel-trade section of the Amalgamated Union of Building Trade Workers; the several relevant sections of the Transport and General Workers' Union; the National Union of Boot and Shoe Operatives; several associations of supervisory staff.

(d) The firms[1] which we asked for information were selected so as to represent various sections of industry and various size groups. Employers were asked to complete a short statistical questionnaire, to give us an interview themselves, and to allow us to interview a number of their employees, including foremen, craftsmen, shop-stewards and apprentices, as well as training officers, works managers and so forth.

The great majority of firms co-operated most willingly. However, the few cases of non-compliance include several important firms. Of the two leading printing firms in Bristol, one refused any information after a preparatory interview; the other filled in the statistical form and let us interview several executives, but not lower grades. The B.A.C., Bristol's biggest employer, also felt unable to permit us interviews other than with high-level managers. We have endeavoured to fill these gaps in the source material in two ways. First, by collecting information outside the firms; in this task we were helped by the fact that many of the big firms' employees and their relatives and friends were met at all sorts of occasions. Second, the restriction of the direct information obtained at the B.A.C. has to some extent been made up by the inclusion in the enquiry of another big engineering works, situated not very far from

---

[1] For simplicity's sake, the word 'firm' is used in this report to denote a single factory or establishment, although in the strict economic sense a firm may own several factories.

Bristol, where we were allowed to interview employees of all grades. The failure by a few other, small, firms to co-operate does not significantly bias the findings.

(e) Every opportunity has been taken for hearing the views of individuals who are in one way or another connected with apprenticeship in the industries under examination, whether or not they were working in one of the firms visited by us. Thus, scores of apprentices from divers firms have been met at certain strategic points;[1] and many meetings and personal contacts have been used in order to hear the opinions of individual craftsmen, shop stewards, supervisors, technicians and executives.

In the course of the investigation we have come across a considerable amount of facts, statistical data, accounts and opinions from other rural areas (including small towns), in Somerset and in neighbouring counties. Significant points from all these intimations are incorporated in the report, and so are pieces of pertinent information gathered at a conference which was attended by delegates from all parts of the country, including the South-West. Statements and comments in this report do not therefore necessarily apply to the areas principally under review. Such a procedure seems justified by the purpose of this enquiry which has been not to give an exact picture of apprenticeship conditions in a particular area but to throw light on the more fundamental problems of apprenticeship in two types of area in the South West.

Whereas we consider with some confidence that the information collected by interview is adequate, this cannot be said regarding the statistical material. Considerable efforts have been made to assemble reliable statistical data on the various aspects of apprenticeship, from sources published and unpublished, official and non-official. The standard of the material from different sources is rather uneven, but on the whole the statistical data relating to apprenticeship have been found to be lamentably poor in quality and quantity.

---

[1] 'Service Open Evenings' of the Bristol Y.E.O., for youths of 18 who have to register for National Service. Day-release classes at technical colleges, by permission of the principals and/or heads of departments. Junior Workers' Meetings of the A.E.U. Boys' Clubs.

INTRODUCTION

APPRENTICESHIP AND OTHER FORMS OF INDUSTRIAL TRAINING

An apprentice is, in the definition of the Oxford Dictionary, a ' learner of a craft, bound to serve, and entitled to instruction from, his employer for a specified term'. This definition helps to some extent to distinguish the apprentice from some other beginners in industry, the learner, the improver and the trainee.

A *learner*, the M.o.L. defined in 1928, is 'a worker who, not being an apprentice, is specifically engaged by the employer for a recognised period of training in the capacity of a learner and is provided by the employer with instruction or with definite facilities for learning a branch or process of the industry.'[1] Some learners are bracketed with apprentices in the administration of deferment under the National Service Acts.[2] However, since learners are trained for semi-skilled occupations, not for skilled crafts, they are not included in our study.

The term *improver* has a double connotation. 'Strictly speaking and in its original significance' it means 'an apprentice who, having completed his term of apprenticeship, is required to serve a further period of training before qualifying for the journeyman's rate'.[3] Thirty years ago, 90% of all apprentices in engineering and 62% in allied industries had to serve an improvership, usually for one to two years. Things are very different today. In most cases, completion of apprenticeship is followed by National Service, and on return to civil life, at about twenty-three years of age, the former apprentice gets full adult wages under the Reinstatement of Employment Acts. It seems worth mentioning however that we found this kind of improvership, i.e. lower than craftsmen's wage rates, forced upon some ex-apprentices who were for medical reasons not called up.

In its second, rather different connotation, the term

---

[1] Ministry of Labour, *Report of an Enquiry into Apprenticeship and Training for the Skilled Occupations in Great Britain and Northern Ireland 1925-26*, VII.—General Report. H.M.S.O. 1928, p.8. Hereafter referred to as *Apprenticeship 1925-26*, The report was made by John Hilton.

[2] e.g. in N.S. 294. See also p.65 below.

[3] *Apprenticeship 1925-26*, p.9.

'improver' is applied to labourers—youths or adults—learning a less-skilled occupation. For example,

'Improvers are to be taken into employment for the purpose of becoming qualified [steelwork erectors]. . . . Three years' experience in the trade is necessary before qualifying for the full adult rate.'[1]

In its first meaning the term improver ranks above that of apprentice, in its second meaning below that of learner.[2]

The term *trainee* is used mainly for novices in non-manual occupations; a drawing-office trainee, for instance, is not indentured; but his training, industrial status and function are difficult to disentangle from that of the apprentice draughtsman; firms were found to include such trainees with apprentices in one statistical return and to exclude them in another return. Moreover, like that of 'improver' the term 'trainee' has acquired more than one connotation. It is also used for craftsmen who are retraining in a firm for a different skilled occupation (e.g. from engraver to electrical fitter), and thirdly for men of any occupation who undergo a craft training at a Government Training Centre.

As will be shown in the discussion of the grading of apprentices,[3] clarity of definition and distinctness is similarly lacking when the term apprentice is applied to full-time university students who are engaged by a firm for intermittent periods of practical training.

HISTORY OF APPRENTICESHIP

The 'origin, history and tradition [of apprenticeship] have exercised so profound an influence on its modern development that it is necessary to refer briefly to them'. This statement from *Apprenticeship 1925-26* remains valid after thirty years. The following are extracts from the historical outline given in that Report (pp.10-14).

---

[1] Confederation of Shipbuilding and Engineering Unions, Handbook of National Agreements, 1949, p.263/4.

[2] 'It implies no definite understanding either as to the length of the improvership period or as to remuneration.' *Apprenticeship 1925-26*, p.9.

[3] P. 87

INTRODUCTION

The long development of apprenticeship may be considered in three phases: (i) Guild Apprenticeship, from the 12th century to 1563; (ii) Statutory Apprenticeship, set up by the Statute of Artificers, 5 Eliz., 1563,[1] and ended by its repeal in 1814; (iii) Voluntary Apprenticeship, since 1814.

The last phase, up to the 1920's, is subdivided into three periods, with these salient features:

(a) the hundred years from 1814 to 1914.

'The repeal of the Statute of Artificers did not involve the disappearance of apprenticeship. . . . It was now, however, a free contract differing in essential features from its predecessor. . . . Towards the end of the period . . . there was a pronounced decline in indentured . . . apprenticeship. The reasons for the decline may be found in the altered conditions of industry. The increasing sub-division and specialisation of processes and the greater use of machinery rendered it unnecessary for many workmen to become acquainted with a complete trade or even a complete branch of trade; with the increase in the size of industrial establishments the obligation on the employer to teach the boy became more remote and in a sense more difficult to fulfil; the speeding up of processes and the increasing use of payment by results made it difficult and even unprofitable for the journeyman to give the time and care necessary for the proper instruction of the apprentice; the competition of boy labour, which under the new conditions had become a source of profit, with that of journeymen led in some trades to the imposition of restrictions by trade unions on the numbers and conditions of employment of apprentices, and in consequence induced a reluctance to employ apprentices.'

(b) the war years 1914-18.

'The causes which, prior to the war, operated to the discouragement of the system of apprenticeship were themselves accentuated during this period and were reinforced by others arising from the liability of boys to be called up for military service. . . . At the end of the war period, therefore, the future supply of skilled men appeared to be seriously menaced. . . .'

(c) The decade after the first world war.

'One contribution towards the reinstatement of the traditional methods of industrial training was made in the Interrupted Apprenticeship

---

[1] Based on a different Calendar System, the year is given as 1562 by some writers.

9

Scheme. . . . The scheme provided . . . where practicable and desirable, for instruction in technical institutions. . . . Important as this contribution was, however, it only affected a temporary phase of the problems of apprenticeship. The sub-division of processes and specialisation in products which had spread to such an extent during the war continued and indeed increased. . . .'

This admirable outline of the history of apprenticeship requires a change of emphasis in one important respect: almost from the beginning of 'Voluntary Apprenticeship' the part played by trade unions has been much greater than is indicated in the outline and indeed by the general tenor of the Report of 1928. More recently, in conditions of full employment and with greatly increased power, trade-unionism has had a major role in the regulation of apprenticeship. This and other matters which constitute the history of apprenticeship in the last three decades will be referred to in this report as occasion arises.

PART I

BACKGROUND AND FRAMEWORK OF THE APPRENTICESHIP SYSTEM

II

THE BACKGROUND

ALTHOUGH apprenticeship today is still 'voluntary' in the sense of not being decreed by statute, its voluntary character is qualified by a number of more or less official instruments and provisions which form the framework of apprenticeship, and also by powerful forces which operate in the background. The two main instruments concerned with apprenticeship are the National Schemes for apprenticeship, which are agreed by the two sides of the various industries, and the individual indentures. But the organisation of apprenticeship can be discerned from these documents only in part. The system is largely determined by uncodified ancient tradition on the one hand, and on the other hand by non-standardized agreements, unpublished customs, tacit 'understandings' and unrevealed procedures which have been developed during the past century.

Ancient tradition is so strong that no clear definition, distinguishing apprenticeship from other forms of learnership, has been deemed necessary, and that no deed of indenture is required for apprenticeship to be recognised as such by the Government, by employers and by trade unions.

If unwritten tradition takes the place of explicit regulation in some apprenticeship matters, in others the procedure has remained uncodified because it is a live issue between employers and trade unions. Questions related with apprenticeship are interwoven in the fabric of industrial relations, and in the continual contest for control of entry into skilled occupations neither side of industry likes to commit itself or to reveal its tactics.

In view of this situation, the following section is concerned with apprenticeship as a social institution. Thereafter we consider in which ways the background of the apprenticeship system has altered consequent on two general developments of great moment: accelerated technological evolution, and changes in the country's educational system since the last war.

APPRENTICESHIP AS A SOCIAL INSTITUTION

'Apprenticeship is the contractual relationship between an employer and a worker under which the employer is obliged to teach the worker . . . and . . . the worker is to serve the employer . . . on stated terms'.[1] Apprenticeship is thus a matter between two parties and, on the face of it, consists of two elements, the reciprocal obligations between the employer and his apprentice. The apprenticeship system, however, has a third element, the function of regulating entry into the skilled occupations; and it involves trade unions as a third party. Hence, also, individual apprenticeship contains a third element, namely the promise of admission to a protected trade.

The first two elements are intrinsic features of the period of apprenticehood (the older word seems more meaningful here); the third, by contrast, arises from post-apprenticehood considerations concerning the craftsman's competitive position in the labour market. Apprenticeship is thus not merely the future craftsman's training for which he pays by bound service; it is also used as a means for other ends, pertaining to the sphere of industrial relations in general.

The interviews for the present enquiry have been focused on the years of apprenticehood and on the problems arising from the conflict of interests of the apprentice and his employer during this period. The regulation of entry into the skilled occupations has been studied by inference rather than in detail, for several reasons: the overt limitation of apprentices is diminishing; the pervasiveness of the indirect interrelations between apprenticeship and restrictive practices was fully realised only in the course of the enquiry; cautious questions

---

[1] *Apprenticeship 1925-26*, p.7.

on this subject which were subsequently put to interviewees met with reticent or evasive answers from both sides of industry and threatened to block the communication which has been readily forthcoming on other aspects of apprenticeship conditions. Glimpses of the interconnection between apprenticeship and restrictive practices were however obtained and, together with the study of older literature,[1] helped to clarify certain baffling features of the apprenticeship system. The very vagueness of one or two recent agreements confirmed these findings.

Until recently three assumptions, whose general validity was taken for granted, underlay the discussion of the regulation of entry into skilled occupations. First, 'regulation' meant the prevention of excess only, not of deficiency of supply of labour; second, the yardstick by which to measure an overstocking of a trade was the employers' demand; third, it was assumed that 'in the main, the employers, desiring a plentiful labour supply, fix the proportion of apprentices to journeymen high'.[2]

Today, the adequacy of all three assumptions has come under fire, though not all with equal justification.

1. Some people fear that industry will be starved of skilled labour because the number of apprentices under training falls short of replacing the present generation of craftsmen. However, as will be shown later, profound changes in industrial methods considerably reduce the strength of this argument.

2. The education and training of each child in accordance with his inclination and ability is now an accepted aim of public policy; thereby a new conception of the proper number to be trained for skilled occupations has come into being, viz. the number of boys wanting, and in the opinion of the Y.E.Os suitable for, an apprenticeship. Even before the imminent bulge of school leavers, the number of applicants for apprenticeship largely exceeds the number of openings offered by firms. The Carr Committee[3] was set up to deal with the problem of the bulge, and in 1958 the Industrial Training Council was established.

---

[1] Most post-war books on Trade Unionism say little on restrictive practices.

[2] J. Cunnison, *Labour Organisation*, p.174 (1930).

[3] A Sub-Committee of the National Joint Advisory Council.

3. Firms' demand for craft apprentices is checked by several factors; (a) many of the traditional crafts have become de-skilled; (b) various jobs which used to be the prerogative of craftsmen can now be given to semi-skilled operatives; (c) apprenticeship is used by trade unions as the basis of demarcation and other restrictive practices. While all three items are treated in some detail in later chapters, item (c) must be briefly considered here, because the organisation and the operation of the apprenticeship system are not intelligible unless the connection between apprenticeship and the vested interests of craftsmen is understood.

The craftsmen's claim to their traditional privileges in the labour market—differential wages and the exclusive right to certain jobs—rests on their having undergone the 'educational servitude' of apprenticeship. Of the two factors, the craftsmen's superiority of education, i.e. of training, has been weakened because of the de-skilling of many old crafts. The other factor, bound service at low wages over a prolonged period, has therefore come to be the paramount argument in the crafts-men's case. It is this consideration, rather than concern with the apprentice's training and well-being during his years of service, which explains the attitude of craft unions and of craft sections in unions such as the A.E.U. to the stipulations and customs which govern apprenticeship conditions.

In a later chapter we shall try to account for the paradox that apprenticeship-based restrictionism is so strong, if largely covert, today, in spite of the decline of craft unionism. But it seems suitable here to deal shortly with the background of trade-union policies of regulating the entry into skilled occupations.

Regulation of entry into occupations has been a prominent feature of the apprenticeship system since medieval times. It was therefore an old policy which trade unions took over after apprenticeship had ceased to be compulsory in 1814. Skilled workers were the first to be organised; and, in the era of free competition, the craftsmen's struggle for better conditions for themselves alone was in tune with the *zeitgeist*. Apprenticeship was the distinguishing characteristic of craftsmen and lent itself to being used for limiting entry into their trades.

Trade-union policy has been informed, said S. and B. Webb,[1] by three divergent doctrines, the doctrine of vested interests, the doctrine of supply and demand, and the doctrine of a living wage. On the whole, they considered, trade unionism has moved away from sectionalism towards collectivism; but they saw the older doctrines still prevailing in some quarters and manifesting themselves in certain trade-union regulations.

By now, the aims of the doctrine of a living wage have been largely achieved, but this collectivist doctrine has not ousted the sectional ones. The two older doctrines are still influential, not least in trade-union policy regarding apprenticeship.

It is the doctrine of vested interests which 'gives the bitterness to demarcation disputes and lies at the back of all the regulations dealing with the 'right to a trade'. It does more than anything else to keep alive . . . the practice of a lengthened period of apprenticeship . . .' These words, written over half-a-century ago, could not be bettered to describe conditions today.

The doctrine of supply and demand is connected with the fact that 'wisely or unwisely, the Trade Unions have tacitly accepted the position that the capitalist can only be expected to find them wages so long as he can find them work'.[2] The engagement of workers is included when the unions recognise 'the right of management to manage'. To further their interests, craft unions resorted therefore to limiting the entry into their trade. Making the supply of craftsmen scarce is a measure to protect them against redundancy; besides, scarcity of craftsmen strengthens their power to obtain monopolistic wages. Limitation of apprentices also has the purpose of checking the substitution of cheaper labour for the craftsman's labour.

Limitation of apprentices is the most obvious form of regulating entry into a skilled trade, but it is of no avail if apprenticeship is not the only gate of entry; hence the craftsmen's perennial fight against the influx of 'illegal men' into their trade. The latter are of two kinds: craftsmen of other trades and non-apprenticed operatives. The craftsmen's defence against the first of these challengers of their exclusive right to the trade is demarcation. Measures against the second are

---

[1] S. and B. Webb, *Industrial Democracy*, p.562f. (1897).
[2] ibid. p.443.

opposition to, or control of, dilution; the rules and practices aimed at controlling dilution are various and varying, and not fully disclosed.

To say that the trade unions' recourse to limiting the entry into skilled occupations was in tune with the conditions and the spirit of the time in the 19th century does not mean that such a policy is sound or justifiable in the different social, economic and technical circumstances of today. This topic will be taken up in a later chapter.

The institution of apprenticeship means different things to different bodies. For trade unions, we have just seen, the main purpose of apprenticeship is the regulation of entry into occupations: it is an issue of critical importance in the sphere of industrial relations.

What matters to the employer of apprentices is to strike a nice balance between training to the standard required for the apprentices' jobs and using the apprentices' services for productive work.

The Ministry of Labour sees in apprenticeship solely a method and opportunity of training. The foremost objects of the Ministry's policy have been, on the one hand, an increase in the number of apprenticeship openings and the improvement of apprentice training, in particular the day release of all apprentices for the attendance at technical courses; and on the other hand, the introduction of some measure of industrial training for all young workers. The aims of the Ministry are indeed praiseworthy. But, if our thesis is correct, the Ministry's policy of resorting to apprenticeship for the training for industry has little chance of success, for it leaves out of account the powerful sectional interests in apprenticeship which undermine its value as a training system.

For the other Government Department mainly concerned, the Ministry of Education, apprentices represent an unspecified proportion of the part-time students at technical and art colleges and at evening institutes.

A popular view of apprenticeship is that it stands for skill and security—a blending of the trade unions' purpose with that of the Ministry of Labour.

APPRENTICESHIP AND TECHNICAL CHANGE

One of the most important factors in the changes that have come over apprenticeship during the past fifty years is the occurrence of numerous and far-reaching changes in technique in practically every industry. These changes in technique have resulted in big changes in the organisation of production and in the job-structure of industry, which have resulted, in their turn, in big changes in the kind of work that industry demands and in the relative proportion of the different jobs demanded.

Fifty or sixty years ago there was, in most industries, a clear-cut distinction between skilled and unskilled jobs. The former required considerable (though not, as a rule, outstanding) intelligence, a very high degree of trained sensitivity of certain senses, highly efficient eye-hand co-ordination, an intuitive knowledge of the properties and behaviour of a certain (fairly limited) range of materials, a familiarity with a rather limited number of types of fundamentally simple machines, together with literacy and an acquaintance with simple arithmetic. The latter required, as a rule, none of these things; they could be done by a person of low intelligence and practically no formal education (F. W. Taylor's 'ox-like man').

Nowadays, the situation is very different. The increased complexity of machines and the greater variety of materials and processes make much greater claims upon the general intelligence, mental alertness and adaptability of the skilled worker ; while at the same time, the increased degree of automaticity of machines, the greater standardisation of materials, and the introduction of scientific tests of quality (for both raw materials and final products) have rendered obsolete some of the craftsman's specialised knowledge, his physical sensitivity and his intuitive 'feel' for machines and materials.

Thus increasing mechanisation and specialisation have led to the de-skilling of many traditional crafts; except for a minority of workers, trades are narrowly specialised. Moreover, the skill which goes into the making of a product has gradually been shifted from the shopfloor to preparatory stages. Generally speaking, in Engineering, the shift takes place within the industry; from Printing and from Building, the skill moves into other industries, mainly Engineering, Chemicals and Professional Services. The locus of the skill which goes into a product has shifted from the shopfloor to the preparatory stages: to work done by technicians (draughtsmen, production, planning and development engineers), by designers and metallurgists, by works managers, estimating clerks, quantity surveyors and so forth. These are the real skilled occupations in modern industry.

These circumstances have called into existence new types of worker. Above craftsmen's level there is now the technician, the man with rather specialised technical training and often proficient in mathematics of a more than elementary nature and literate in no mean degree. Above the technician comes the technologist. These semi-professional and professional occupations have been drawn into the apprenticeship system to a large extent and with far-reaching implications. The apprenticeship system now embraces future technicians and technologists, even some scientists, and various managerial specialists.

Technicians and professional workers of this sort form a very small fraction of the total labour force of modern industry. The bulk of the workers belong to a category that has largely replaced the old-style skilled craftsman. They are intelligent, alert, adaptable and literate; but lacking in many of the hardly acquired skills of the old type of craftsman. Such a man, if he has the necessary inborn qualities, can be trained for a particular job much more quickly than the old-style craftsman.

The supply of workers of this category has taken place in two ways. On the one hand, the more intelligent and adaptable of the unskilled workers have been trained to work on the new machines and processes and have been promoted to 'semi-skilled' status, without undergoing a formal apprenticeship. On the other hand, men who have gone through a formal apprenticeship are employed on the new machines and processes and do, in fact, perform work that is essentially of the same type as that of the semi-skilled man. Concurrently, the kind of training given to many apprentices under modern working conditions has changed gradually from one appropriate to the training of the old-style craftsman to one appropriate to training a 'one-skill' man or a 'semi-skilled' worker. In other words, over a wide range of industry, the old-type skilled craftsman has disappeared and been replaced by a man who is essentially of the type now known as semi-skilled. Whether he is called 'skilled' or 'semi-skilled' depends upon whether he has gone through a formal apprenticeship or not; the actual nature of his work is the same.

There is still a demand, though a limited one, for the services of the old type of craftsman. He is still needed in small factories, particularly those doing special or non-routine jobs, and in some large factories where pioneer and development work is being done and in some cases of production directly for the customer. Thus this type of worker still survives. But the continuance of the species is a problem. There are not many firms nowadays which can spare the time and trouble, or which have the resources, to train such a worker. However, the former mechanic has a successor in one modern engineering occupation: the ever-growing mechanisation throughout industry has created a demand for maintenance engineers in a great number of firms in many non-engineering industries.

At the bottom of the scale, new methods of production (mechanisation, handling devices, etc.) have greatly reduced the need for the old-style unskilled labourer and, together with recent improvements in primary and secondary-modern education, have enabled the former unskilled worker to develop into a much more intelligent and adaptable type. There is no real boundary separating workers of this type from the 'semi-skilled'.

The demand of industry is now, therefore, for four categories of skill:

(a) nominal absence of skill, which is by no means incompatible with intelligence and handiness;

(b) one-job skill, required of the major proportion of the labour force;

(c) craftsmanship in the old sense (precision work and all-round competence); the demand for this grade of craftsman is relatively much reduced;

(d) technicians' proficiency (draughtsmen, planning

engineers etc.) the demand for which is greatly on the increase.

The boundaries between these categories are fluid and changing: the actual hierarchy of skills no longer corresponds to the conventional labels that are attached to the various grades of worker.

Change in requisite skills has been, and will continue to be, so rapid and far-reaching that the number of apprentices required to meet the future needs of industry can no longer be estimated by reference to the present number of craftsmen in the various trades. It would be a mistake to apply today a standard suitable under static conditions, viz. apprentice ratios 'capable' of maintaining the existing number of journeymen'.[1]

'CREAMING OFF' AND THE EDUCATION ACT OF 1944

The changes brought about by the Education Act of 1944 are another development with a close bearing on the apprenticeship system. While formerly apprenticeship was far and away the most important road to a satisfactory career for gifted working-class boys, nowadays intellectually talented children of all families receive grammar-school education. This 'creaming off' of the ablest (in terms of 'measured intelligence[2]') fifth or fourth of the pupils has the corollary of lowering the average ability of modern-school leavers from whom apprentices are traditionally recruited. This fact need not however be accepted in a spirit of resignation; it can be accepted as a challenge: 'The great future problem of education generally, and of technical education in particular, will be to produce workers of higher quality out of less promising material'.[3]

[1] The words in quotation marks are from *Apprenticeship 1925-26*; but the Carr Report ' *Training for Skill : Recruitment and Training of Young Workers in Industry*, (1958) still argues along similar lines.

[2] See, however, J. E. Floud (Ed.), A. H. Halsey and F. M. Martin, *Social Class and Educational Opportunity* (1956), p.143: 'There are still marked differences in the chances which boys of different social origins have of obtaining a [grammar-school] place. . . . The problem of inequality of educational opportunity is . . . not disposed of.'

[3] A. B. Clegg and J. M. Hogan, 'Technical Education' in *Researches and Studies*, The University of Leeds Institute of Education, January, 1956, p.16.

At the same time, the apprenticeship system has been extended to the training of technicians and technologists, and these higher-grade apprentices are recruited from grammar schools and secondary technical schools.

III

THE FRAMEWORK OF APPRENTICESHIP

THE framework of apprenticeship is two-fold, one frame applying to the age-old industrial side of apprenticeship, including practical training, the other to technical education, which is a recent development; in addition, the framework receives support from the Deferment Board and from the Youth Employment Service.

INDUSTRIAL

Until quite recently, the only formal instrument regarding apprenticeship was the indenture. Since the end of the last war however, National Schemes for apprenticeship have been agreed upon by the National Joint Bodies of employers and trade unions for various industries or sections of industry; the Ministry of Labour and also the Ministry of Education take part in the negotiations through the Central Youth Employment Executive (C.Y.E.E.).[1] Each industry has thus a particular apprenticeship framework, consisting of the individual indenture and the industry's National Scheme.

[1] The composition of the C.Y.E.E. is described on page 41 below. Agreed Schemes are issued under the heading 'Recruitment and Training of Young Persons for Industry' in a series of supplements to the C.J.E.E. Memorandum No. 3 (The letters stand for the original name which was Central Juvenile Employment Executive). The Memorandum and Supplements have now been superseded by a C.Y.E.E. Information Handbook which is issued to the Youth Employment Service; particulars of new Schemes are published from time to time in the Ministry of Labour Gazette.

The indentures of the various industries are markedly alike. It is convenient to show at first only the features which they have in common, leaving their differences to be discussed later, because these differences are due largely to the fact that the indentures are geared to the industries' National Schemes; also, a difference may be only one of phrasing—see p.29n.

The Indenture or Deed or Agreement[1] of Apprenticeship is a contract between the individual employer and the individual apprentice and his guardian. This document (which retains much of its medieval form and phrasing) embodies the fundamental features of apprenticeship: the apprentice, by his own signature and that of his guardian, binds himself to serve the employer for a specified number of years; the employer undertakes to teach the apprentice a given trade; and, most important for the apprentice, provision is made for the endorsement of the indenture: 'when the apprentice has served the employer to the satisfaction of the latter for the full period of service a certificate to that effect will be given to the apprentice by the employer';[2] in other words, after five years, the apprentice becomes a craftsman entitled to a 'skilled ticket' of his union.

Apprentices' conditions of work and rates of pay are now laid down in the general National Agreements for the various industries, and in the indenture, both employer and apprentice undertake to abide by them.

The National Schemes for various industries have a few almost identical clauses, but in many respects they differ significantly. Features common to all National Schemes for apprenticeship[3] are of two kinds: one, ancient and binding, the other, new and discretionary. The first group consists of the stipulation of long-term service (usually five years) and of rigid

[1] Despite the legal difference between a deed (which is sealed) and an agreement (which is not), Apprenticeship Agreements in the engineering industry are generally referred to, and in the working of the apprenticeship system recognised, as ' indentures'.

[2] Agreement form of Engineering and Allied Employers' National Federation; similar phrasing in other indenture forms.

[3] As stated in the introduction, we are concerned with apprenticeship in the strict sense, i.e. excluding learnership and other forms of industrial training. The inclusion of the latter in the C.J.E.E. series ' National Schemes ' is discussed on p. 43 f.

age limits for beginning and completion of apprenticeship (usually 16 and 21 years respectively); clauses of the second group were included in the Schemes at the instigation of the Ministry of Labour, particularly those on day release for technical education, on the formalization of apprenticeship by deed or written agreement, and on collaboration with the Youth Employment Service.

Excepting the few binding clauses which they have in common, the National Schemes of different industries vary greatly both in comprehensiveness and in the strictness with which the various topics are treated. At one extreme, regulations are detailed and mandatory, at the other extreme, vague and optional: topics may find no mention; measures may be recommended but not enjoined; stipulations may be so indeterminate and hedged in by qualifications as to be quite non-commital; finally, measures agreed upon may remain on paper.

The contrast between strict and loose schemes does not imply that the former are good and the latter bad schemes: rigid application of a bad or out-dated rule is just as deplorable as is the omission or evasive phrasing of a useful stipulation.

If we compare the apprenticeship framework in the three industries under review, we find in Printing and Engineering two schemes quite opposite in character. The apprenticeship Scheme in the printing industry is uniform, comprehensive, rigid and restrictive; that in the engineering industry multifarious, loose and desultory and compatible with great unevenness and with change and experiment. The apprenticeship Scheme of the building industry occupies an intermediate position in this respect.[1]

In order to bring out the characteristics of the apprenticeship framework in a given industry, we have to answer three questions: what topics are dealt with? what is the actual regulation regarding each topic? and what is the degree of stringency of each regulation?

---

[1] The order in which the three industries are dealt with in this report varies : we start in each section with the industry which presents the simplest or the most complete picture of that section's subject.

THE FRAMEWORK OF APPRENTICESHIP

Printing
The National Scheme for apprenticeship in Printing and
Bookbinding[1] makes the following provisions:[2]

Administration: the Scheme is controlled by a joint Apprenticeship Authority for the industry and operated by Local Joint
Committees.

Selection of apprentices: to be a function of the Local Committee:
individual firms to recruit from boys thus selected. Method
set out and strongly recommended by the Apprenticeship
Authority. Collaboration with the Y.E.S.: recommended.

Probation: a period of three months may precede apprenticeship, counting as part of it.

Indenture: a three-party agreement between the employer, the
guardian and the apprentice is recommended.

Trades for which apprenticeships are available: about twelve
trades (there are local variations) are listed; strict demarcation.

Ratio of apprentices to journeymen: ratios are maximum ratios
and are separate for individual trades and for individual firms;
they are mostly 'on a sliding scale which reduces the ratio as
the number of journeymen increases'; stringent.

Age of entry into apprenticeship: 15–16. 'The length of the
apprenticeship discourages entry at much over 16'.

Age of completion: normally at age of 21 or a little over;
apprenticeship must not terminate before 21 years of age;
categorical.

Length of apprenticeship: five to six years; minimum of five
years: coercive.

Practical training: specimen syllabuses of training have been
prepared by the industry's Apprenticeship Authority and are
'brought to the notice of all employers of apprentices'.

Technical education in day-release courses: 'release for one day a
week for attendance at trade classes is strongly recommended
but is, at present, not a condition of apprenticeship.'

The general character of the printing apprenticeship Scheme
is particularly shown up by two of its clauses. The designation
of the industry's national joint apprenticeship council as

[1] Scheme No. X, C.J.E.E. Mem. No. 3, Supplement No. 2 and amendments.
[2] Order of clauses and phrasing of the several Schemes are slightly altered for
the sake of comparability.

Apprenticeship Authority points to uniformity and coerciveness: and the employers' agreement to severe limitation of apprentices by discriminative ratios indicates the power wielded by the printers' unions.

Engineering

In contrast with the Scheme for printing apprenticeship, that for apprenticeship in the engineering industry is strikingly casual. It reflects the conditions in a growing and developing industry, where there is a great disparity between firms as to what sort of apprentice training may be expected from them; further it reflects a persistent trial of strength between employers and trade unions regarding apprentices and apprentice-trained craftsmen. If the apprentice scheme of the printing industry manifests the dominance of the printers' unions, the scheme of the engineering industry indicates by its very sketchiness that on various important matters no national agreement has been reached between employers and workers.

While there is a separate National Scheme for apprenticeship in Shipbuilding and Repairing, nearly all the other sections (a very heterogeneous collection of trades and industries) of the Engineering and Allied Industries are covered by one National Scheme for apprenticeship.

The National Scheme for apprenticeship in the engineering industry[1] is loose. There is only one definite stipulation in the whole document, viz. 'In no case . . . shall the apprenticeship end before the age of 21'. In addition, normal craft apprenticeship is affirmed to begin at 16 years and to end at 21 years of age; but allowance is made for boys of more advanced education to begin apprenticeship at a higher age, still completing it when they are 21. In fact, 21 years is made both the minimum and the maximum age limit for completing apprenticeship in most trades.

Topics not mentioned in the engineering Scheme are: selection; probation period; apprenticeable trades; apprentice ratios. Topics recommended but not made mandatory are: written agreements and day release up to 18 for attending technical courses. Topics hedged in by such qualifications as

[1] Scheme No. XIII, C.J.E.E. Memorandum No. 3, Supplement No. 3.

'a measure of' and 'as far as possible' are: transfer to another employer; and, most important, workshop training beyond that sufficient for a one-skill job. A measure agreed upon but not implemented in the S.W. Region is the establishment of local apprenticeship committees for the engineering industry. The National Joint Body was to lay down, and seek the adoption of, minimum standards of training; instead, it has recommended optimum standards in the form of detailed specimen syllabuses of training which 'it has been suggested . . . would be welcomed . . . [as] general guidance'. 'It is appreciated', the syllabuses state, 'that the facilities and the type of work available in different firms vary so greatly that . . . firms will require to arrange the details of training and periods of time to suit their particular circumstances or requirements.' (See p. 89).

The indentures, too, are quite vague as regards the training of apprentices in the engineering industry. (Firms may have their own indenture forms printed, but most use forms issued by employers' associations). The employer will 'permit the apprentice to enjoy the advantage of acquiring . . . to such extent as is practicable, having regard to the conditions of work and of organisation from time to time existing in the works or in the particular department thereof . . . a practical knowledge of the trade of . . . . so far as from time to time that trade is being carried out in the works and the capacity and proficiency of the apprentice admits'. Technical education is left to the employer's discretion in the indenture form of one employers' association, while in that of another it is not mentioned at all.[1]

While indentures, or at least written agreements, are the rule, there are still firms that do not give written indentures but whose apprentices are recognised as such both by Government departments (see for example p. 42, below) and by the two sides of industry. And the training given by such firms may actually be well above the average. The value of the indenture is discussed in the chapter ' Completion of Apprenticeship.'

[1] Engineering indentures stipulate that apprentices shall not take part in labour disputes. Printing and Building indentures make this stipulation implicitly: the apprentice must not without the master's consent absent himself from his service. The stipulation is now without practical importance in big engineering works but still important in printing houses.

Building

The building industry was the first one to have a National Apprenticeship Scheme. In 1943, the Ministry of Works appointed a Building Apprenticeship and Training Council, an advisory body with a membership representing employers and workers, professional and educational institutions and several Ministries.[1] Based on the Council's recommendations, an apprenticeship scheme emerged which is in various respects a model of its kind; the question is whether some of the stipulations are realistic or whether they are rather counsels of perfection.

The National Scheme for apprenticeship in the building industry[2] which came into operation in 1945 dealt with most of the topics covered in that for printing apprenticeship, leaving out only practical training, and including three other stipulations, viz. on registration, on certification and on transfer or cancellation of apprenticeship. Whereas the headings were thus similar, the general emphasis was different; in one important matter the difference has been acknowledged in a revision of the Scheme of the building industry. The original Scheme had a clause on the ratio of apprentices to craftsmen, phrased however as a desideratum, not as a mandate ; the revision, in 1953, deleted the clause, and 'no ratio . . . is now laid down.'[3] On the other hand, attendance at technical courses, both during working hours and on two evenings a week, the latter during the whole term of apprenticeship, is firmly enjoined on building employers and apprentices; the minimum age of entry into building apprenticeship is, in S.W. England, 15, and that of completion is 20, as against 16 and 21 years as the usual minimum ages of entry and of completion respectively.

An outstanding feature of the scheme is the establishment of a national register of all apprentices in the building industry. Until 1953, apprentices were enrolled with the Council set up by the Ministry of Works. Now, the whole scheme is

---

[1] B.A.T.C. *Final Report* (1957) para. 2.
[2] Scheme No. IV, C.J.E.E. Memorandum No. 3, Supplement No. 2.
[3] ibid, Supplement No. 12.

administered by the industry's National Joint Apprenticeship Board which had been established under the Scheme.

For indenture, a standard deed of apprenticeship is prescribed and is therefore uniform for the whole country and all building firms. The building indenture is a four-partite deed, a representative (an employer) of the Local Joint Apprenticeship Committee being the fourth signatory in addition to the three usual parties—master, apprentice and guardian. This representative is given important functions: before he signs an indenture he must not only be 'satisfied that the apprentice is a suitable person . . . ', but also have 'enquired into the nature of the business conducted by the master'. The latter provision aims at ensuring that employers of apprentices are qualified to train them; this is an effort to make good an astonishing deficiency of the prevailing apprenticeship system: since the abolishment of statutory apprenticeship in 1814, a person requires no qualification for taking on apprentices. The training progress too is made subject to enquiries by the representative of the Local Joint Apprenticeship Committee.

The building indenture's clause on technical education is detailed; it makes the same exacting, specific and binding stipulations as the National Scheme: the master has to undertake to release the apprentice up to 18 on one whole day (or two half-days) a week, and the apprentice undertakes to attend not only these day classes but in addition evening classes twice a week during the whole period of apprenticeship.

A new clause (though the practice is not new) has been inserted in the building industry's deed of indenture: since October 1955, apprentices have specifically to covenant that they will claim deferment of call-up for National Service.[1] To make such a covenant a condition of apprenticeship does not seem quite in line with the provisions of the National Service Acts under which the youth himself has the right to decide whether to claim deferment of his call-up.

The National Apprenticeship Scheme's high standards as to education and to administration have prevented the Scheme from becoming comprehensive. To begin with administration, the Scheme is devised to cover the building industry, not the

S.W. Federation of Building Trades Employers, Yearbook 1955, p.286.

building trades. An industry-based Scheme is obviously expedient for such measures as registration, transfer of an apprentice to another master, and supervision by Local Joint Apprenticeship Committees; but it means (with certain exceptions) the exclusion from the Scheme of those building-trade apprentices who are employed by non-building firms, hospitals, local authorities etc., in their maintenance departments.

A much greater weakness of the Scheme, however, is its imperfect acceptance within the building industry. A considerable number of firms, mainly small builders, oppose the National Scheme and train apprentices under arrangements outside the Scheme. A major cause of this situation is the Scheme's rigorous requirements as to technical education: small builders find the day-release stipulations of the National Scheme too great a burden. Moreover, at least one organisation of small builders with thousands of member firms resents that they are not represented on the National Joint Apprenticeship Board. Last, but not least, many small builders are not prepared to adhere to the demarcation between trades which is laid down in the National Apprenticeship Scheme.

Some figures showing the incomplete coverage of the National Apprenticeship Scheme are given in the chapter ' The Number of Apprentices'.

GRADING OF APPRENTICESHIPS

Short mention must be made here of apprenticeship grading. The printing industry and the trowel trades have only one grade of apprenticeship, the trade or craft apprenticeship (these two terms are being used as synonyms). In the engineering industry, however, a system of several grades is developing.

Apprenticeships of higher grade than craft apprenticeship were mentioned in the *Apprenticeship 1925-26* (on p.88) in 1928. What was then a small beginning has now become a major factor of apprenticeship in the engineering industry. The traditional trade apprenticeship is still the predominant one, and it is the only grade offered by the great majority of engineering firms. But big firms, and some not so large, have been erecting a super-structure of higher grades, determined by higher educational standards at the beginning of apprenticeship, and/or by superior practical and technical instruction, and by wider prospects at its completion.

Of the few firms in our area which have apprenticeship of more than one grade, almost each one has a slightly different set of tiers—different in the number of tiers, in nomenclature, or in the levels at which the distinction of grades is made. The apprentice grading of various firms will be discussed in the Part 'The System in Operation'. The industrial framework acknowledges the existence of several grades implicitly rather than explicitly,[1] but apprenticeship grading has to be mentioned here, because it is linked with the differentiation of technical courses which is a prominent feature of the educational framework.

EDUCATIONAL

Since practical training is arranged within the industrial framework, the educational framework of apprenticeship refers to technical education only. It concerns three matters: day release for attendance at technical courses; provision of technical colleges; and different types of courses and examinations.

DAY RELEASE

The term 'day release' connotes that the employer allows the apprentice to attend a technical course during working hours without loss of (time-rate) wages.

Technical education is not a condition of apprenticeship, and the intention of the Education Act, 1944, to make part-time education after the statutory school-leaving age compulsory for all young workers up to the age of 18, has not so far

---

[1] The syllabuses of training approved by the two sides of the engineering industry are meant for those apprentices 'most of whom are likely to continue as craftsmen during their working years', thus implying the existence of apprenticeships which lead to higher positions.

been implemented. However, as already stated, the National Schemes of the several industries recommend or demand attendance at day-release courses by all apprentices up to 18 years.

The specification of 18 years as the age after which technical education ceases to be urged upon apprentices and their employers was not arrived at in consideration of the particular requirements of technical education; 18 years was simply the age laid down in the Education Act of 1944, as the upper limit of statutory further education in general.

The age at which technical education is to begin is not mentioned in any of the National Schemes under review, but they imply that day release for technical education starts when apprenticeship starts. Where the minimum age of entry into apprenticeship is 16 years, as in the main engineering trades, there are thus at most[1] two years available for part-time technical education before the apprentice's 18th birthday.

Another relevant point is the 'educational gap' in the life of boys who enter employment at 15 but start apprenticeship and technical education only at 16 years of age. Such a lag is not a new phenomenon. Thirty years ago, it was described as 'a feature of modern apprenticeship which has frequently been deplored . . . '[2] A fuller implementation of the Education Act, 1944, would fill the hiatus; but the statutory school-leaving age has not been raised to 16, nor has further education up to the age of 18 been made compulsory. For a great number of boys, therefore, the gap persists; and being left for a year or more without systematic education at the age of 15 is perhaps an even greater handicap in the pursuit of technical knowledge than in the development of the apprentice's other faculties.

In Printing, in Building and in one or two 'minor' engineering trades, the minimum age of entry into apprenticeship and

---

[1] The time is shorter for apprentices who are 16½ at the beginning of the technical college's annual session and who stay away as soon as they are 18.

[2] *Apprenticeship 1925-26* p.76.—However, the lag between entering employment and entering apprenticeship is much older than the introduction of compulsory education in modern times. Long before the days of factory labour, when children began to work at a very early age, 'in the best trades and [gilds] children were not taken as apprentices until the age of twelve or fourteen at the least'. O. Jocelyn Dunlop, English Apprenticeship and Child Labour: A History, p.98 (1912).

of the beginning of technical education is 15 years. In these trades, therefore, the educational framework provides for technical day-release courses to link up with full-time secondary education without a long interruption. How far this and other arrangements are actually carried out by different industries, firms and apprentices is another matter, as will be shown in the part 'The System in Operation'.[1]

The National Schemes of many industries define the amount of time to be devoted to technical education during the working hours as 'The equivalent of one day per week'. In most cases, employers actually release their apprentices on one day each week. But in some industries, including engineering and building, an alternative form of day release is developing; the time for technical education, at least equivalent to one day a week, is bunched into periods varying from several months to one week. These sandwich courses, block-release and one-week-in-four schemes are still in various stages of experiment, although block release (without this name) had been provided for in the Education Act of 1944 for attendance at county colleges.[2]

TECHNICAL COLLEGES

Nearly all technical colleges (this term is used as a generic one, including large colleges of technology as well as small technical institutes) are maintained by local education authorities. The responsibilities of L.E.As to provide facilities for further education are still limited—up to 1944 they had no binding duties in this respect. The shortage of places is such that most of these colleges 'were full soon after they opened and have been bursting at the seams ever since.'[3] Such great demand for admission to technical colleges would not have arisen without the championing of apprentices' technical education by the Ministry of Labour and National Service: it has been the policy of the Deferment Board to offer a strong incentive to day release.

---

[1] Chapter 7, pp. 115 ff. and passim.
[2] See p. 119 below.
[3] White Paper on Technical Education, 1956, para. 26 (Cmd. 9703).

Apprentices whom their employers release during working hours usually attend one day per week; many attend one or two evenings as well, the attendance at evening classes being often made a condition of day release. In Bristol, apprentices whose education is not up to the requirements of the technical college can attend the Day Continuation School (D.C.S.) where technical subjects are taught along with English and other subjects; the D.C.S. does not distinguish between apprentices and non-apprentices among its pupils.[1] The Day Continuation School is a rudimentary step towards the County Colleges which were to be established under the Education Act, 1944 (Section 43) in that it provides for a measure of liberal education after the statutory school-leaving age. The courses at the technical college include at most a modicum of non-technical education. The D.C.S. relieves the technical college in two respects, in reducing the pressure for places and in raising its minimum educational standards.

Apprentices who are not given day release by their employers can attend classes after working hours, either in technical colleges or in Evening Institutes; the latter are usually on a lower level.

Beside the L.E.A. technical colleges, which cater for apprentices of all firms in the area (and beyond), another type of technical college has come into being, viz. the Company or Works School of a large firm; such a school is adapted to the particular requirements of the respective firm; but the Ministry of Education has an amount of control over works schools, since they are grant-aided.

TYPES OF COURSES AND EXAMINATIONS

Technical education of craftsmen had developed since the middle of the 19th century under the influence of examinations conducted by the Government's Science and Art Department and by the City and Guilds of London Institute. The former examinations were discontinued in 1918[2] but the City and Guilds (C. & G.) examinations and syllabuses continue to

---

[1] See p. 123, footnote, for recent re-organisation.
[2] *Education 1900-1950:* Report of the Ministry of Education for 1950, p.49.

determine one of the two streams of technical education of apprentices. The other stream is the system, developed from 1921 onward, of courses and examinations for National Certificates.

City and Guilds Courses and Examinations

There are over 150 subjects in which syllabuses are published by the Institute and examinations held (at local technical colleges); 74 of the subjects pertain to the three industries under review, viz. 12 to Printing, 17 to Building and 45 to Engineering and allied industries.

In some subjects, the C. & G. Certificate is obtained by a single-grade examination, but in most subjects, there are an intermediate and a final examination, the first of which can be taken after at least two, but more frequently after three years' part-time study, the second after four or five years. A candidate successful in the final examination is awarded a Final Certificate of the First or the Second Class according to the standard he attains in the examination.[1] Each examination consists of two papers, each of three hours' duration; to give an example, in Patternmaking, one paper is in the main on pattern-making practice, the other on drawing, geometry and calculations.

A 'Full Technological Certificate' can be taken in certain subjects in all three industries under review after a further two years' part-time study. These Certificates are based on study over a wider field than the lower-grade certificates; in typography, e.g., a compositor has to pass a qualifying examination in machinists' work, and a machine-minder in compositors' work.

The kind and amount of knowledge aimed at in the courses may be illustrated from the C. & G. Note of Guidance.[2]

'It is not essential that the patternmaker should be familiar with the metallurgical aspect of foundry work. It is, however, very essential that he should have a thorough knowledge of the various operations and principles involved in the preparation of a mould.'

[1] C. & G. of London Institute, Regulations and Syllabuses, Department of Technology, D.1955-56, p.59.   [2] ibid., p.42.

The C. & G. syllabuses are 'examination syllabuses', showing the field covered in examinations; but the technical colleges are invited to draw up their own syllabuses for the courses so as to insure the best order of sequence for purposes of instruction and to allow for local industrial differences.

For apprentices in the printing industry, C. & G. certificates are all that exist, outside a few important centres of printing, of which Bristol is not one; in those centres, advanced courses leading to diplomas are held. But for a number of engineering subjects and for a few others, including building, the C. & G. courses and examinations have been supplemented by a system of more advanced, more scientific and more theoretical courses and examinations. In Bristol, trowel-trade apprentices rarely take the higher course in 'General Building'; they attend City and Guilds courses in Brickwork and in Plastering respectively. In engineering, however, the higher courses have come to play an important part in the technical education of apprentices.

National Certificate Courses and Examinations

The National Certificate system has been developed, since the end of the first World War, by the Ministry of Education in co-operation with the various professional institutions.[1] The courses were meant to cater for 'the higher, more professional grades of part-time education',[2] in view of 'the need of industry for a body of well-trained technicians and professional men.'[3] In actual fact, many craft apprentices attend N.C. courses. These courses constitute, therefore, part of the framework of apprenticeship in general.

Two grades of National Certificates are awarded: the Ordinary National Certificate (O.N.C.) and the Higher National Certificate (H.N.C.). Examinations can be taken after three and five years respectively.[4] The certificates are granted jointly by the Ministry and by the professional institution(s)

[1] Institution of Mechanical Engineers ; Institution of Electrical Engineers, etc.
[2] P. F. R. Venables, *Technical Education*, p.154. (1955).
[3] Ministry of Education, Report for 1950, p.49.
[4] There are deviations from this general pattern (the H.N.C. in Civil Engineering takes six years, for instance), but it seems unnecessary here to describe such details.

concerned, and the technical colleges are represented on the Joint Committees for the schemes. National Certificate schemes[1] in engineering and related subjects exist now in :—

Subject	Year of Introduction
Mechanical Engineering	1921
Chemistry	1921
Electrical Engineering	1923
Production Engineering	1941
Civil Engineering	1943
Applied Physics	1945
Metallurgy	1945
Applied Chemistry	1947
Chemical Engineering	1951

The Ministry of Education issues Rules on the 'Arrangements and Conditions for the Award of National Certificates' in the various subjects. Under these rules, schemes for courses are prepared by a technical college (in response to local industrial needs), but have to obtain the joint approval of the professional institution and of the ministry. The matters on which approval of a scheme depends include not only the curriculum and syllabuses of instruction; the courses must also be carried on for a stipulated minimum of hours per year, and it is a condition of the award of a certificate that the candidate makes at least 60% of the total attendance in each subject in each year as stated in the approved scheme.   Further,

'before approving a scheme ... the Institution and the Ministry will require to be satisfied ... as to ... the steps to be taken [by the college] to secure that students are not admitted to the courses unless they are qualified to profit by them.'[2]

But this clause remained a dead letter for many years; the lingering disregard of so crucial a stipulation is discussed in the chapter on Technical Education (passim).

A very important attribute of the National Certificates is that they pave the way to professional status. The holder of the H.N.C. requires certain 'endorsements', confirming a pass in an examination in ancillary subjects which he may take in

---

[1] Higher Diploma Courses fall outside the scope of this study.
[2] M.O.E. Rules 106 (Mechanical Engineering), clause 4.

one subsequent year, to become a Graduate member of the appropriate professional institution.[1]

SUPPLEMENTARY

Several Government Departments have assisted in constructing the apprenticeship framework. We have already referred to the leading role of the Ministry of Works in setting up a modern apprenticeship scheme for the building industry; to the collaboration of the Ministry of Education in the initiation of National Certificate examinations; and to the participation of the Ministry of Labour in the negotiations on National Schemes for apprenticeship in various industries. In addition, the apprenticeship framework receives continuous support from the Youth Employment Service and from the Deferment Board.

THE YOUTH EMPLOYMENT SERVICE

All three National apprenticeship Schemes under review contain clauses envisaging co-operation with the Juvenile (as the term then was) Employment Service—the Schemes were agreed before the present Y.E.S. was established by the Employment and Training Act, 1948.[2] Under the Act the Service is to be provided for all persons under the age of 18 years. Schools are required by statute to supply the Y.E.S. with reports on all pupils likely to leave school at the statutory leaving age, but in respect of older school leavers there is not yet such a statutory obligation.

The foremost function of the Y.E.S. is to give vocational guidance; further functions of the Service are the placing of young persons in employment and review of progress, i.e. follow-up work.

Administratively, the Y.E.S. is a dual system, operated

---

[1] He has, however, ' . . . to gain a position of sufficient responsibility before he becomes eligible for the Associate Membership'. P. Venables, *op. cit.*, p.158. (N.B. The Associate Membership of the various engineering Institutions is the normal qualification that confers full professional status).

[2] The Act is based on the (Ince) *Report of the Committee on the Juvenile Employment Service* (1945).

partly by the Ministry of Labour, partly by education authorities. The dualism is less pronounced at national level: the Central Youth Employment Executive, while staffed by officers of the Ministries of Labour and of Education and of the Scottish Education Department, is responsible to the Minister of Labour. But locally, the Y.E.S. is a function of the Ministry of Labour only where Local Education Authorities have not opted to conduct the service.[1] In Bristol, as in other large towns, the Youth Employment Office is part of the City's Department of Education. Elsewhere in the survey area, including the 'fringes' of Bristol, Youth Employment Officers are attached to local Employment Exchanges or to the Bristol Employment Exchange.

THE NATIONAL SERVICE DEFERMENT BOARD

The National Service side of the Ministry of Labour and National Service contributes greatly to carrying into effect the apprenticeship policy of the Ministry's civil side.

The normal age of call-up for National Service has until recently been 18, and is now 19 years; but apprentices may apply for deferment of their call-up until after the completion of their apprenticeship. The decision lies with the Deferment Board.

Most apprentices appear to desire deferment, except in printing where the normal six-year apprenticeship is reduced to five years if national service is taken during apprenticeship.[2]

The great majority of employers are very keen on the deferment of their apprentices' call-up. Some firms stipulate in the indenture that the apprentice is to apply for deferment when he registers for National Service, although the firms have no

---

[1] The Minister of Labour defrays 75% of the approved net expenses of a L.E.A. incurred in the administration of a Youth Employment Scheme. The grant is, however, a composite grant, covering also the costs of the work connected with Unemployment Benefit and National Assistance which Y.E. Officers perform as agents of the Government. See Seventh Report from the Select Committee on Estimates, Session 1956-57: 'The Youth Employment Service and Youth Service Grants', Minutes of Evidence, Q.195.

[2] C.J.E.E. Memorandum No. 3, Supplement No. 6: amendment of National Scheme.

legal right to do this. Such formal stipulation is not common,[1] but in fact firms usually see to it that their apprentices apply for deferment.

The general eagerness for deferment gives the Board considerable influence on apprenticeship conditions, and it exercises this influence to press in particular for indentures or other written agreements of apprenticeship and for apprentices' attendance at technical courses during working hours. A youth who is indentured and who attends technical classes normally qualifies for deferment. But there are on the one hand spurious indentures, and, on the other hand, genuine apprenticeships without a written agreement and without day release. Such cases are investigated before the call-up is deferred. Furthermore, deferment is granted initially for 12 months only, and before it is renewed, the Ministry of Labour's Technical Officers examine, where doubt exists, whether the apprentice's training continues to be satisfactory.

In these ways, the importance of minimum standards of apprenticeship conditions is brought home to lads, parents and employers. Often, it is true, if deferment is refused, which in the nature of the situation occurs to a youth of nearly 18 or over, it is too late to put things right for the individual—he may be too old to be admitted to a recognised apprenticeship. Such pathetic cases turn up at the 'National Service Open Evenings' of the Youth Employment Office. In the long run, however, the refusal of deferment in bad cases is bound to improve apprenticeship conditions.

Whether the Board's scrutiny goes sufficiently deep under the surface is a different question. However that may be, the Deferment Board plays an important part in raising apprenticeship standards, particularly by promoting day release for technical education. It is therefore imperative that this valuable function of the Board should be made the responsibility of some other body when National Service, and with it the Deferment Board, comes to an end.

---

[1] Except in the building industry—see p. 31 above.

THE FRAMEWORK OF APPRENTICESHIP

A Note on the National Schemes for Recruitment and Training of Young Persons for Industry

National Schemes for apprenticeship are published in a series of Supplements to C.J.E.E. Memorandum No. 3. This series contains all National Schemes for recruitment and training, not only apprenticeship schemes, and the schemes for apprenticeship *stricto sensu* are mixed indiscriminately with schemes for learnership, for traineeship, or for a modicum of initial training for all 'entrants . . . at ordinary operative level' (Wool; similarly in Surgical Dressings and several other industries.)

Besides, in many National Schemes the term apprenticeship is used quite loosely, viz. applied to the training for occupations which are not skilled crafts in the accepted sense[1]; there is, for instance, provision for a three-year apprenticeship for animal-gut workers and for an apprenticeship of two years' maximum duration for kerbdressers in Roadstone Quarrying.

It is a much reported fact that over one hundred National Schemes have been established. But this number does not tell us much; the 'industries and sections of industry' in which Schemes have been agreed to not conform to any existing industrial classification and cannot, therefore, be related to a total number of industries and sections of industry. Of the many incongruities in the listing of National Schemes the following are illustrations. There are two Schemes each, for England and Wales and for Scotland respectively, in Agriculture, Slaughtering, Electrical Contracting, and Radio Servicing. While one countrywide Scheme covers Engineering in general, there are two separate Schemes, for Sewing Needle Manufacture and for Surgical Needle Manufacture, both concentrated in the Redditch area. Several important industries figure once or even twice in the list of National Schemes, but not with reference to the occupations specific to the industry. Thus, Coalmining has two Schemes, for the training of mining surveyors and of maintenance engineers respectively, but none for the training of miners; similarly, Cotton's two Schemes cover only loom-overlookers and staff trainees; the training of textile technicians, but not that of textile workers, is the subject of National Schemes in the Silk and Asbestos industries. The schemes of some

---

[1] i.e. not, to use the American term, apprenticeable trades. In Germany an approved list of apprenticeable trades is kept up to date by the Central Office of Vocational Training (Birmingham Productivity Association, Gaining Skill . . ., p. 13; 1955).

industries, contrariwise, cover a wide range of their employees: an agreement signed in 1947 in Boot and Shoe Manufacturing provided for the training of 'entrants, learners, students, operatives and other employees and principals'; in 1955, however, an extra scheme was adopted for intensive planned training of selected operatives (boys and girls) for posts of higher responsibility. A number of schemes concern such occupations as dental technicians, laboratory technicians, opticians and junior journalists; hospital cooks, catering cooks, jockeys, hairdressers and film projectionists account for another five National Schemes.

The wording and the manner of listing of the National Schemes invite misinterpretation in various respects. The most frequent form is a statement that over one hundred schemes have been agreed, with the implication that the number is a high one, whereas in fact it is meaningless.

PART II.
THE SYSTEM IN OPERATION

IV

THE NUMBER OF APPRENTICES

THE first thing one would wish to know about the apprenticeship system in operation is the number of apprentices. But the available statistical information is rather poor.

For England and Wales as a whole we have the following numbers in 1951:[1]

Male Apprentices and Articled Pupils in All Occupations	351,315

In Metal Manufacture and Engineering (excluding Engineering Draughtsmen) ..		176,555
Engineering Draughtsmen (est.)[2] ..		8,800
	(est.)	185,000
Printing and Bookbinding		15,722
The Trowel Trades (excluding Masonry)		18,904
viz. Bricklaying .. 15,773		
Plastering .. 3,131		
	(est.)	220,000

The three groups of apprentices with which the present enquiry is concerned totalled roughly 220,000 and accounted for nearly two-thirds (62%) of the male Apprentices and

---

[1] Census 1951, Occupation Tables.

[2] Viz. some 3,000 engineers listed under Professional and Technical Occupations plus one-half of 11,546 draughtsmen ' not elsewhere specified'.

Articled Clerks in all occupations, the engineering group alone accounting for over one-half (52%). These figures are given here because they indicate the order of magnitude; the actual numbers are of limited use for our purpose in view of the lapse of time since the Census was taken and also because the classification differs in several respects from that of other statistical information on apprentices.

Building

At first sight, the number of building apprentices appears to be readily available, since the National Joint Council for the Building Industry keeps a National Register of Apprentices and a local register is kept for the Bristol area.[1] On 30th September 1956 the number of apprentices registered in the Bristol area were:

All Building Trades		Bricklayers		Plasterers	
No.	%	No.	%	No.	%
706	100	129	18.3	47	6.7

In fact, however, these figures give a very incomplete picture of the apprentice strength in the building trades. An unknown number of building trade apprentices is not on the register, namely those who are not indentured under the building industry's apprenticeship scheme; these fall into two categories. First, there are the building-trade apprentices who are employed in the maintenance departments of non-building firms, local authorities, hospitals, etc. The apprentices of some of these departments are on the Register, but others are not. The only indication we have of the number of the latter in Bristol is that 124 of them are students in the Building Department of the College of Technology. Second, a fact of much greater import: as already mentioned, many apprentices are employed by small firms under arrangements which are 'leading to craft ability and status'[2] but do not conform to the National Scheme; these de-facto apprentices are therefore not on the National Register and are described as 'non-indentured

---

[1] This Area includes not only Greater Bristol, but also Clevedon U.D., four neighbouring Rural Districts in their entirety and considerable parts of four others.
[2] B.A.T.C., *Final Report*, para. 28.

learners', although 'it is claimed that many of the individual arrangements fall only a little way short of the national requirements.' While no local figures on these non-registered apprentices are available, figures for the country as a whole are shown annually by a Ministry of Works Census.[1] In September 1955, the proportion of 'apprentices (sic) . . . under verbal agreements', i.e. not on the National Register, was 37·4% among bricklayers and 40·6% among plasterers. The corresponding proportions in other building trades were 41·8% for carpenters and joiners, 53·8% for plumbers and glaziers, and 63·4% for painters; in all building trades together (excluding electricians), the proportion of apprentices serving under verbal agreement was 46·8%; in other words, apprentices on the National Register accounted for not much more than one-half of the total.

For all we know, the proportion of apprentices on the Bristol-Area Register may be considerably higher than the national average; but it is obvious that statistics of registered apprentices are of limited significance. Besides the available statistical material is not of a kind and quality which would make tabulation advisable. Even so, some conclusions emerge from the analysis of the data which we obtained from the Local Joint Apprenticeship Committee and from the Building Department of the College of Technology, together with the Ministry of Labour's size-coding of firms. These findings indicate that the local distribution of building-trade apprentices conforms to the pattern in the country as a whole: (a) apprentice training is mainly done by medium-sized firms; (b) even among the firms employing apprentices under the industry's National Scheme, i.e. excluding the host of small builders who remain outside, the small firm predominates; (c) connected with points (a) and (b), the number of apprentices per firm is small; the bearing of this situation on apprentice training will be discussed in Chapter 6.

The building firms interviewed by us and furnishing statistical information are shown in the table on the next page. Before we come to it, however, it seems apposite to emphasize

[1] ibid., Appendix 6: Number of Craftsmen and Apprentices employed by firms making returns (Ministry of Works Census).

a point (made in the Introduction) on the range of our interviews in general. With few exceptions, our interviewing of firms was not confined to one spokesman: in addition to a director and/or manager of a firm we interviewed employees of all ranks, including apprentices. Moreover, factual information was obtained also from firms whose statistical information was insufficient for their inclusion in the table. By the interviewing of firms without apprentices, light on certain problems of apprenticeship was thrown from another angle.

The table shows that our small sample of firms conforms to rule in that medium-sized firms take a very big share in apprentice training. The particularly high proportion of apprentices to craftsmen in firm B3 reflects the determination of a new director to raise the standards of craftsmanship and morale in the firm. The concentration of apprentice plasterers is on the whole characteristic; but in the degree of concentration in one firm (B5), our small sample is not representative: it is estimated that about one-half of the apprentice plasterers in the Bristol area are employed by this firm.

NUMBER OF APPRENTICES IN BUILDING FIRMS INTERVIEWED BY US
IN ORDER OF SIZE (TOTAL EMPLOYEES)

Total Employees Size Group*	Firms	Craftsmen	Apprentices		
			Total	Brick-layers	Plasterers
F	B1	375	62	14	4
E	B2	372	51	13	4
D	B3	73	45	19	––
	B4	103	35	16	—
C	B5	61	20+	—	20+
B	B6	30	10	4	—
	B7	†	3	1	—
A	B8	21	4	1	1
	B9	22	6	1	1
	B10	18	2	1	—
X	B11	8	2	1	—

* Ministry of Labour Size Groups

No. of Employees :

F—*1,000 or more;* E—*500–999;* D—*250–499;* C—*100–249;*
B—*50–99;* A—*20–49;* X—*under 20, no M.o.L. coding.*
† Information refused

The number of apprentices registered with the Bristol Joint Apprenticeship Committee excludes apprentices who are brought to Bristol temporarily by large non-Bristol firms—the Building Department of the College of Technology sometimes gets a few of such apprentices as students for a year or two and then sees them wandering off again. The existence of such transient apprentices points to a characteristic of the building industry which has important bearings on apprenticeship openings in the building trades. Building differs from manufacturing industries in that the locus of its activities changes; when one contract is completed, it may be years before another one turns up in the same locality, except maintenance and repair jobs. Large building firms therefore tend to set up in big centres and, in addition to doing business there, to send out their skilled labour now to one place, now to another, according to where they secure orders. Small towns and rural areas are devoid of substantial building firms. Bristol stands between the extremes. On the one hand, the larger Bristol building firms, including one specialising in plastering, send their craftsmen to work on contracts in smaller towns and villages; on the other hand, especially in times like the present, when the reconstruction of Bristol's bombed business areas is being tackled (but also for the building of council housing in recent years), some of the biggest contracts go to giant non-Bristol, mostly London, firms; these establish ephemeral Area Offices here,[1] and there is a temporary influx into Bristol of their keyworkers, and of a very small number of apprentices.

Local boys are rarely taken on as apprentices by outside firms which operate in Bristol only temporarily. In the prevailing conditions of immobility of labour, such a firm will be chary of signing the deed of a five-year apprenticeship with a local boy, unless the building contract in Bristol is expected to take at least five years; transfer to another employer, when the original one moves his operation to a different area, is provided for in the industry's apprenticeship scheme but would deprive the first

---

[1] The current (1957) issue of the Bristol Telephone Directory contains such non-Bristol firms as Costain's, Holland & Hannen's, John Laing's and Wimpey's; McAlpine's have now left the City, having completed a contract after several years' work.

employer of the apprentice's most productive years, in the later part of his service.[1]

The fact that itinerant building firms take on few local apprentices must be considered as contributing to the scarcity of apprenticeship openings in the building trades. For the country as a whole, the local deficiencies of apprenticeship openings in the various areas where firms from London and other large towns obtain building contracts must add up to an over-all shortage of such openings. This aspect of building contracts going to outside firms has until recently attracted little attention[2] (in contrast, for example, to local employers' bitter complaints about the poaching of adult craftsmen by the 'pirate' firms).

If the 'national' firms contribute to the deficiency in openings for apprenticeship, so do the lowest units in the industry, the 'labour-only' gangs; these consist of two or more bricklayers or plasterers to whom building firms sub-contract. Labour-only gangs are not firms, they have no fixed address; they do trowel-trade work, but it is in the nature of their unstable existence not to take on apprentices. The gang has functions similar to those of the 'single installation' craftsman in the printing industry, but whereas the compositor to whom a printing house sub-contracts the setting of type owns a Monotype or Linotype machine, the labour-only gang in the trowel trades has the raw materials and scaffolding provided by the contractor. Trade unions are bitterly opposed to labour-only sub-contracting, because it undermines their strength for collective bargaining. Some building firms disdain to deal with labour-only gangs; others, though they may decry them as the ruin of craftsmanship, yet employ them 'to even out fluctuations'.

The sub-contracting of building work to labour-only gangs is

---

[1] The joint secretary (employers' side) of the Bristol Joint Apprenticeship Committee argued that Bristol firms would not like to have such older apprentices transferred to them because they would have learnt different methods and, if trained by large firms, would be narrowly specialised.

[2] In the Final Report of the B.A.T.C., however, it is pointed out that 'many of the largest contracting organisations in the industry find themselves unable to make a proportional contribution to the training of apprentices on account of the very wide-spread nature of their activities. The lack of continuity of their work in one area prevents recruitment of apprentices, who are not normally sent to work away from their homes area'. para. 85.

not a new practice[1]. Today it is so wide-spread as to alarm the trade unions concerned: in 1955, the matter was discussed at the annual conference of the Amalgamated Union of Building Trade Workers (the trowel trades' Union). In the employers' journal we find: 'the National Apprenticeship Scheme is clearly inoperable under labour-only sub-contracting, and it is an interesting question as to how far the paucity of apprentices —especially in the Southern half of the country—is due to this cause'.[2]

Printing

In spite of minute control over the intake of printing apprentices (described in chapter five) the data available on the apprentice strength in Bristol are neither as accurate nor as detailed as one could wish. But they are sufficient to show the order of magnitude of the apprentice strength of Bristol's printing industry, viz 300 odd.

The figures (overleaf) were obtained from the Bristol branches of the several craft unions; but they do not all cover the same area.[3] The numbers include the journeymen and apprentices at present in the Forces—the ratios are calculated on this basis—but only for the T.A. is their number available (35 journeymen and 36 apprentices were away on National Service). Another difficulty is that apprentices do not generally join the Union in their first year of apprenticeship (T.A. and S.L.A. mention this[4]), so that the number of apprentice members of the trade unions would seem to understate the total number of apprentices. Attempts to improve on the trade-union figures were unavailing, but produced the interesting intimation that about half of the T.A. apprentices are compositors and half, machine minders; this compares with a proportion among adult journeymen of

[1] 'For nearly half a century we have used in relation to our sub-contracts the sheet anchor of the Fair Wages Resolution of the House of Commons, but we are now having difficulty'. Mr. J. Armstrong, *Trades Union Congress Report*, in 1955, p.464.

[2] *The Builder*, 14th October, 1955, in an article reproduced in *The Operative Builder*, The Journal of the National Federation of Building Trades Operatives, January-February, 1956, p.14.

[3] Some, for instance, include Paulton with the large firm of Purnell's, others do not.

[4] See p. 151 below.

roughly 2 : 1. The difference in proportion seems to confirm the observation made by one of our informants that nowadays about equal numbers of compositors and of machine minders are required, because the keyboard machines make composing work so much quicker than it used to be.

PRINTING

NUMBER OF JOURNEYMEN AND OF APPRENTICES BY TRADE

Members of Trade Unions, Bristol Branches, 1956

Trade Unions	No. of		Ratio
	Journeymen	Apprentices	(1) / (2)
	(1)	(2)	(3)
Typographical Association Compositors Machine Minders	1,275	164	7.8
Society of Lithographic Artists Litho Artists	154	38	4.1
Process (Letterpress) Workers	72	18	4.0
Photogravure Workers	25	11	2.3
	—— 251	—— 67	—— 3.7
Amalgamated Society of Lithographic Printers	284	56	5.1
National Society of Electro- typers and Stereotypers	56	14	4.0
Bookbinders and Machine Rulers (Craft section of N.U.P.B.P.W.)	60	17	3.5
Total	1,926	318	6.1

The last column of the table shows how the ratio system operates in Bristol. As an example of the nationally agreed ratios, those for compositors may be given, i.e. the number of compositor apprentices allowed to a firm employing a given number of compositor journeymen:[1]

1 Journeyman	1 Apprentice(s)	
3 Journeymen	2	,,
8 ,,	3	,,
18 ,,	4	,,
40 ,,	5	,, + 1 for every additional 20 journeymen.

The ratios for the other printing trades are similarly regressive: the ratio becomes rapidly less favourable to firms as the number of their journeymen increases. The apprentice ratio of the T.A. (compositors and machine minders taken together) shows this impressively. Whereas this ratio for E. & W. as a whole[2] is 1 : 5·4, for the Bristol branch which includes three very large printing firms it is only 1 : 7·8. This proportion of apprentices to journeymen in the T.A. is considerably lower than that in other printing unions in Bristol, and the average Bristol proportion is one apprentice to 6·1 journeymen.

While the sliding scale of the agreed ratios discriminates against firms with many journeymen, such firms' apprentice entitlement is often increased to some extent through their using several different printing processes operated by journeymen of different trades. Since the ratios are both regressive and applied to individual trades, the apprentice entitlement is higher for a firm employing, say, 10 journeymen of one trade and 10 of another, than it is for a firm employing 20 journeymen of a single trade. The apprentice ratio system thus encourages larger firms to use more than one printing process.

In the following table, the printing firms which gave us statistical information are arranged in order of total employees. From this, the order of journeyman strength (col. 2) deviates in one case: firm P2 has a very high proportion of semi-skilled

---

[1] British Federation of Master Printers : ' Basic Wages and Conditions ' 1954, p.65; these basic ratios remained unaltered in the 1956 Agreement when the T.A. granted a fixed 'bonus' of apprentices, viz. 545 apprentices for the whole country above the ratio 'entitlements' and whose admittance was to be spread over three years.

[2] But practically excluding London, where the T.A.'s place is taken by several specialised unions.—Source: T.A. half-yearly Report, September 26th, 1955 to March 31st, 1956.

workers, employed mainly in stationery manufacture; in numbers of journeymen, P2 ranks below P3. If this is taken into account, it can be seen that, on the whole, the apprentice ratio (col. 4) increases as the number of journeymen decreases; the gradient would be steeper but for the use of different processes in the larger firms; the irregularly low ratio in firm P3 reflects the lack of differentiation of that firm's printing work; firm P8, on the other hand, does not use its full entitlement of two apprentices.

Number of Apprentices in Printing Firms interviewed by us in Order of Size (Total Employees)

| M.o.L. Size Group* | Firms | Journeymen Number | Apprentices† | |
			Number	Ratio (2)/(3)
	(1)	(2)	(3)	(4)
F	P1	477	66	7.2
E	P2	108	18	6.0
	P3	195	25	7.8
C	P4	73	13	5.6
	P5	49	10	4.9
B	P6	26	6	4.3
X	P7	10	3	3.3
	P8	5	1	5.0

* Ministry of Labour Size Groups: see * on p. 50.

† Excluding non-printing craft apprentices of various categories: paper-box trade apprentices; design and editorial trainees; also maintenance engineers and carpenters.

Engineering

In the engineering and allied industries, there is no registration of apprentices, and no reliable figures are available. The order of magnitude however is known: whereas the apprentice strength in the printing and the building trades in the Bristol district is to be counted in hundreds, that in the engineering and allied trades runs into thousands; it seems a safe estimate to put the number at well over 3,000.[1]

Knowledge of the total number of apprentices would make possible a judgement whether the number is sufficient for the replacement of the present generation of craftsmen. But far-reaching changes in technology and in the occupational structure have lessened the importance of this question. What we want mainly to know is the distribution of apprentices: the proportions trained for various occupations, including non-manual ones; the spread of apprentices over the various and so diverse sections of the industry; further, the numbers of apprentices in establishments of various size. This last point is important for the understanding of the whole situation, as the basis of realistic recommendations. The question is: do the numbers of apprentices employed by big and small firms respectively bear out the frequent statement that small firms do not do their share in the training of apprentices, but rely on engaging men trained by large firms? if so, the situation would

[1] This estimate, for 1955/6, starts from the following data :

	Number
B.A.C. apprentices (*)	1,175
Day-release students, Engineering Department, College of Technology (*)	1,400
Apprentices employed by engineering firms who attend Day Continuation School	265
	2,840

(*) About 200 B.A.C. apprentices who attended courses at the College of Technology are included in the B.A.C. figure and excluded from the College figure.

The total of 2,840 is the sum of the complete number of B.A.C. apprentices and of an unknown proportion of the apprentices in engineering trades employed by other firms. The number of day-release students at the College (the small contingent at the D.C.S. can be left out of account here) does not cover the apprentices who have discontinued attendance at day courses after reaching the age of 18; their number is unknown, and so is the number of apprentices who do not attend day courses at all (see Chapter VII,' Technical Education'). On the other hand, it is true, the College of Technology has in its higher courses some students from firms outside the Bristol district, e.g. a few from Wells and from Chippenham, but they are, no doubt, greatly outnumbered by the Bristol apprentices of the above-mentioned categories who do not, or no longer, attend day courses.

Because of the various inevitable omissions, the total number of apprentices in engineering and allied trades in the Bristol district must be assumed to be considerably higher than 2,840, the result of our rough approximation.

be the reverse of that stated in the *Apprenticeship 1925-26* to have prevailed thirty years ago.[1] But both parts of this comparison need close scrutiny. As to the first, the statistical evidence on apprentice distribution among engineering firms in 1925/26[2] on which the statement is based is, to say the least, inconclusive, because a high proportion of the smaller firms were either not included in the enquiry or did not complete the questionnaire, whereas most of the principal firms submitted returns; and it is reasonable to assume that the small firms from which no information was received had few if any apprentices.

As regards the present, the situation is intricate. Too little is known of the occupational structure of firms, beyond the fact that such 'unproductive' workers as draughtsmen and production engineers are of increasing numerical importance.

Our enquiry into this matter raises more questions than it answers, but one negative statement can be made: our information does not corroborate the assertion that the number of apprentices employed by large firms is disproportionally high.

This conclusion is based not only on the data which we collected directly but also on the results of a regional apprentice survey which were put at our disposal.

For our enquiry, fifty firms were asked to give information regarding apprentice engineers. Two small firms did not reply, two others refused (one of them stating that no apprentices were employed). 46 firms agreed to co-operate and were interviewed. Of these, six had no apprentices (all of them small) and four were non-engineering firms. Two firms had to be omitted from our table because of lack of statistical information.[3]

The remaining 34 firms have a total labour force of about

---

[1] 'There is indeed a clear inference from the figures that among firms taking apprentices it is the smaller rather than the larger firms which in proportion to their size do most in the way of training boys for the skilled occupations'. This observation was made on industry in general, but Engineering was explicitly given as an example. Ministry of Labour, Enquiry into Apprenticeship 1925-26, Vol. VII, p.25ff.

[2] ibid., Vol. VI—Engineering . . . Industries, pp. 5/6 and 10.

[3] Three other firms failed to return our statistical questionnaire, but sufficient numerical information was obtained in the interviews for these firms to be included in the table.

40,000 and the number of their apprentices is over 2,000. The size of individual firms ranges from many thousands to 6 employees. By the Ministry of Labour's size classification, the size distribution of the 34 firms with apprentices is as follows:

Size of Firm	X	A	B	C	D	E	F
Total employees	Under 20([1])	20–	50–	100–	250–	500–	1,000 & over
No. of firms	2	8	5	5	4	5	5

The main products of the various firms are as different as aircraft, precision machinery, electronic equipment, industrial motors, gears, sheet metal and constructional ironwork. Some of the premises are old, some new, some in the centres of city or country town, others on the outskirts.

Well over half of the total apprentices in these firms are employed by the Bristol Aeroplane Company; the apprentice strength of our sample of 34 firms is distributed in this way:

			Firms with . . . Apprentices				
Under 5	5– 9	10– 19	20– 49	50– 100	100– 199	200– 1,000	Over 1,000
No. of firms 7	6	7	6	6	1	—	1

Relative apprentice strength is traditionally measured by the ratio of apprentices to craftsmen. This method is straightforward where all, or nearly all, apprentices are trained to become craftsmen; today, however, there are in addition apprenticeships of higher grades which lead to non-manual occupations. If the higher-grade apprentices are included in the calculation of apprentice ratios, their adult counterparts should also be included; but it is difficult to define, and to obtain reliable figures of, the latter. The next-best procedure is to compute craft-apprentice ratios only, i.e. to omit from the calculation apprentices of higher grades[2], who will become

---

[1] Not size-coded by M.o.L.   [2] see p. 85ff, below.

technicians, technologists or managers, and to relate the number of craft apprentices to the number of adult craftsmen.[1] This ratio is shown in col. (3) of the table overleaf.

The average ratio in the 34 firms is 1 : 7·2; in individual firms, it ranges from 1 : 1·2 to 1 : 28·0. In 14 out of the 34 firms, the ratio is one apprentice to between 3 and 5·9 craftsmen; seven firms have ratios higher than 1 : 3; on the other end of the scale are seven firms where the ratio is lower than 1 : 10. No correlation between size of firm and apprentice ratio is apparent. Firms of similar size have very dissimilar ratios; thus in four firms with between 500 and 800 employees each the ratios are 1 : 2·7, 1 : 3·3, 1 : 4·9 and 1 : 11·8, and this not in either ascending or descending order of size of firm; three firms with between 100 and 150 employees each have ratios of 1 : 1·9, 1 : 3·4 and 1 : 12·5; of seven firms in the size group 20-49 employees, two have ratios of about 1 : 1·2, two of around 1 : 3·4 and three of 1 : 10 or lower. The four largest firms in the sample have low apprentice ratios: as regards apprentice training for craftsmen's jobs, the large firms' contribution is below the sample's average of 1 : 7·2.

Higher-grade apprentices, by contrast, are to be found mainly in large firms, and there can be little doubt that in the training of apprentice technicians and technologists, large firms are far and away in the lead.

A comparison of firms' training of apprentices of all grades was attempted by the aforementioned regional apprentice survey.

The synopsis of the returns of well over a hundred firms gives separate figures for Craft apprentices, Engineering apprentices and Student apprentices. A juxtaposition of the numbers of Craft apprentices with the numbers of skilled adult manual workers shows, just as our sample of firms does, that the apprentice ratio is not a function of size of firm. There are low ratios (say, one apprentice to ten or more skilled men) in quite

---

[1] It is true that the deduction of higher-grade apprentices from the total apprentice strength of firms with formal grading leads to overstating the proportion of apprentices trained by smaller firms because a few of the latter's Craft apprentices eventually become designers, managers and so on. But the resulting bias cannot be great, for even in terms of 'inclusive' ratios (see p.61f.) most large firms are below the average.

APPRENTICE RATIOS IN 34 ENGINEERING FIRMS INTERVIEWED
BY US, IN ORDER OF SIZE

| Size of Firm | | Firms | Apprentice Ratios | |
M.o.L. Size Group	No. of Total Employees		One Craft Apprentice to . . . Craftsmen	"Inclusive" Ratio*
	(1)	(2)	(3)	(4)
F	1,000 or more	E1	9.3	6.1
		E2	8.5	5.6
		E3	28.0	19.2
		E4	14.6	10.5
		E5	4.4	3.5
E	500–999	E6	4.8	
		E7	6 †	
		E8	4.9	
		E9	2.7	2.3
		E10	11.8	8.7
		E11	3.3	
D	250–499	E12	5.3	2.5
		E13	9.0	
		E14	4.5	
		E15	4.3	3.8
C	100–249	E16	2.7	
		E17	12.5	
		E18	3.4	
		E19	1.9	
B	40–99	E20	4 †	
		E21	4.5	
		E22	5.2	3.9
		E23	1.2	
		E24	1.4	
A	20–49	E25	1.2	
		E26	10.0	
		E27	1.1	
		E28	14 †	
		E29	3.6	
		E30	3.3	
		E31	3.5	
		E32	10.0	
X	Under 20	E33	6.0	
		E34	5.0	
	Total 34 Firms		7.2	5.5

* Column (4) is discussed on p. 62.   † Estimated on the basis of verbal information.

a few large firms, and high ratios (say, one apprentice to three or fewer skilled men) in quite a few small firms.[1]

But this is not how the apprentice ratio was calculated for presentation of the survey results: the procedure was to relate the total of apprentices of all grades to the number of craftsmen employed. There is thus a failure to relate like to like ; while the number of apprentices includes the Engineering and Student apprentices all of whom 'are training for what we [one of the biggest firms] regard as professional or semi-professional occupations', the number in the adult group is restricted to skilled manual workers. The ratios are therefore over-stated, and since higher-grade apprentices are heavily concentrated in large firms, their apprentice ratios are apt to be grossly over-stated in comparison with the smaller firms' ratios.

In order to show the difference made in the ratio by the inclusion of higher-grade apprentices without a corresponding alteration of the adult group, we give in column (4) of the preceding table the 'inclusive' ratio (as it may euphemistically be termed) for the firms in our sample which have more than one apprentice grade. In firms E1 to E4 and in some smaller ones, the 'inclusive' ratios are about one-third higher than the craft-apprentice ratios, the fact being that in each of these firms about one-third of all apprentices are Engineering or Student apprentices. In firm E12, apprentice draughtsmen outnumber craft apprentices; hence, the 'inclusive' ratio is more than twice the other.

For clarity's sake an entry is made in column (4) only for those firms whose 'inclusive' ratio differs from their craft-apprentice ratio; for the other firms the entries in column (4) would be the same as in column (3). The average 'inclusive' apprentice ratio of the 34 firms is 1 : 5·5. Even by this calculation, the apprentice ratios of the largest firms are below the average. The synopsis of the regional apprentice survey provides evidence of the same situation.

If our tentative conclusion is correct, viz. that the size of a

[1] This statement cannot be made in definite numerical terms, for two reasons: (a) the firms giving information are a self-selected sample of uncertain coverage ; (b) the numbers of firms' total employees are not made available. Our statement in the text is based partly on knowledge from other sources of some firms' size, partly on inference.

firm is not the decisive determinant of its apprentice ratio, the question arises what other factors are accountable. Our material shows that a high apprentice ratio may have very different causes: a new or expanding and/or awkwardly located firm may train a proportionally large number of apprentices because it has difficulty in engaging sufficient craftsmen of the required skill. On the other hand, some firms employ apprentices in order to use them as cheap labour rather than to train craftsmen—witness this remark by a managing director: 'with the number of apprentices we have, we obviously would not want them all to come back to us after military service' (when they are entitled to skilled men's wages). Again, there are firms with a high proportion of semi-skilled workers: the apprentices they train are intended to provide foremen for the semi-skilled departments in addition to craftsmen working on the shopfloor. Foremen are excluded in the calculation of apprentice ratios both from our material and from that of the regional survey, and this procedure has different effects on the ratios of firms with different job structure.

The foregoing observations show the need for detailed research into the occupational composition of engineering firms so as to make possible a proper assessment of their apprentice strength.

V

RECRUITMENT, SELECTION AND PROBATION

THE YOUTH EMPLOYMENT SERVICE

RECRUITMENT and selection may be said to begin with the Youth Employment Service (Y.E.S.). Whereas a firm's recruiting is concerned with the interest of the employer, the prime concern of the Youth Employment Officer (Y.E.O.) is the interest of the future employee.

Since the last war, conditions of full employment in general and of scarce juvenile labour in particular have meant that Y.E.Os have had no difficulty (barring a few problem cases) in helping school-leavers to find employment of some sort. Indeed, the big demand for young workers has absorbed even boys and girls of small competence who would in other conditions be unplaceable. This is one of the reasons for complaints about the alleged low educational level of the average modern-school leaver.[1]

But short supply of juvenile labour in general does not mean that there are sufficient openings for apprenticeship. In the survey area, supply of recruits for apprenticeship has greatly exceeded demand, even before the imminent 'bulge' of school-leavers.

No realistic figures on apprenticeship openings are available. The annual analysis of Young Persons Entering Employment appears at first sight to show that both in 1955 and in 1956 37% of all boys entering employment between 15 and 18

---

[1] Another reason is the creaming off of the brightest fifth or more of the children who are now receiving grammar-school education.

entered apprenticeships to skilled crafts.[1] But this high proportion is arrived at by a rather wide and somewhat wishful definition of apprenticeship: 'apprenticeship to skilled craft' includes, together with apprenticeship proper and actual, learnership and also employment 'likely to lead to apprenticeship at a later date'. The inclusion of learners ignores the accepted meaning of the terms apprenticeship and skilled craft.[2] The inclusion of likelihood of apprenticeship at a later date makes overstatement almost unavoidable: we found it a not infrequent practice of engineering and of building firms, both large and small, to recruit as potential apprentices many more 15-year olds than they intend to apprentice.[3] Only a part of these will actually become indentured, but when they start work and give their particulars for the statistical return to the Y.E.O. issuing their first National Insurance Card, all may state correctly that they have the prospect of apprenticeship.

The much quoted figure of 37% must therefore be regarded as a considerable overstatement. But even by this sanguine reckoning, the majority of boys entering employment under 18 years of age have to go into non-skilled occupations. In other words, from the school-leaver's point of view, the problem of apprenticeship lies in the first place in the scarcity of openings. From the employer's point of view, on the other hand, the problem is the qualitative one of finding apprentices of the right calibre.

Apprenticeship is so highly valued by parents and boys that they are liable to be unconcerned with quality and breadth of training and of future work. Y.E.Os endeavour to increase parents' discrimination between good and bad employers, but in view of the scarcity of openings for apprenticeship, they cannot easily, or even may not consider it right to, dissuade boys from binding themselves as apprentices to unsatisfactory employers.

The chief task of the Y.E.S. is vocational guidance which 'must be based on adequate information about the young

[1] *Ministry of Labour Gazette*, October, 1956, p.362, and October 1957, p.357f.; the proportion was similar in the preceding years.

[2] A special case might be made out for learners in building crafts ; see above, p.48f.

[3] See p.78 and p.79.

person on the one hand and a knowledge of job requirements on the other'.[1] The National Youth Employment Council has with increasing emphasis urged the importance of Y.E.Os acquiring themselves and disseminating knowledge about the various occupations and industries. The influence of the two talks which Y.E.Os give to boys and girls during their last year at school cannot be measured, but teachers confirm their value, not only by the actual information they give but also by the general interest they arouse in those addressed, and indirectly throughout the school. The talks are followed by individual interviews for which the Y.E.O. is provided with a school report of each child. In addition, industrial visits for school children are arranged, and printed information is given in the 'Choice of Careers' booklets which are prepared by the Central Youth Employment Executive. The C.Y.E.E. also screens the literature on careers published by would-be employers of juvenile workers. The contact which the Y.E.S. establishes between school-leavers and their potential employers presents indeed a great progress, considering that thirty years ago the world of the Elementary School and the world in which the young worker moved touched at hardly any point.[2]

In the several ways just mentioned it is intended to build up in the young person's mind 'a broad picture of the various fields of employment and of their demands upon his abilities and personal qualities'.[3] However, in view of the amount of dissatisfaction which we found among apprentices, the question arises as to how realistic that picture is in the sphere of the apprenticeable trades where de-skilling and shift of skill have wrought so far-reaching changes.

If we envisage all industrial occupations arranged in order of skill, the unskilled at the base, the most highly skilled at the apex of a pyramid, craftsmen are today somewhere in the middle. In the past, master craftsmen had formed the top, but in modern industry layers of professional and semi-professional occupations have come to be superimposed on the craftsmen's

[1] *The Work of the Youth Employment Service 1953-1956.* A Report by the National Youth Employment Council, p.6.

[2] (Malcolm) *Report of the Committee on Education and Industry* (England and Wales), Second Part, p.48 (1928).

[3] *The Work of the Y.E.S. 1953-1956*, p.6.

layer. At the bottom end, the stratum composed by craftsmen extends now downwards to lower skills; the skill required of one-job craftsmen is not much superior to that required of semi-skilled operatives.

Thus, skill has moved up into new occupations and has diminished in the lower stretches of the traditional crafts. To this shift, the scope of the apprenticeship system has been adjusted in one direction but not in the other. Technicians (and even some technologists) have been drawn into the apprenticeship system which now reaches up into the semi-professional occupations and beyond. For them, apprenticeships of higher grade than craft apprenticeship have been introduced. The de-skilling of many traditional crafts, on the other hand, has not led to a withdrawal of the lower boundary of the apprenticeship system. De-skilled jobs continue to be counted as 'skilled men's work', and boys are apprenticed for such trades which do not entail much training.

The Y.E.S. has responded eagerly (though there is unevenness between areas)[1] to the upward extension of the apprenticeship system; it will suffice here to mention the work of the Service for grammar-school pupils. But too little cognizance is taken of the change at the lower end of apprenticeable occupations, viz. of the decline of interest and skill attaching to them. In other words, there is a failure to disabuse the minds of would-be apprentices and their parents of the prevailing idea that apprenticeship of whatever kind means all-round training for craftsmanship in the traditional sense.

That boys in fact enter apprenticeship with mistaken expectations is exemplified by the bitter comment of an apprentice indentured as a machinist—one of many similar complaints: 'Lads are taught one branch of machining only; this is not our idea of being a machinist.' The Choice of Careers booklets, which may stand for the attitude of the Y.E.S. as a whole, are meant 'to present a fair picture, stressing the good points but including unpleasant features . . . and avoiding all forms of recruitment bias'.[2] The booklets do mention eventual specialisation, but not many boy readers will be made aware of

---

[1] See p.184ff below.
[2] *The Work of the Y.E.S. 1950-53*, p.15.

the narrowness of training for, and of the monotony of, one-skill jobs from the variety of descriptions and illustrations of 'the kind of jobs that an apprentice bricklayer learns' or of 'the kinds of job that fitters, turners and skilled machinists do'.[1]

We have here one of the causes of apprentices' disappointment, frustration and consequent indifferent work. The Y.E.S. would seem to have particular opportunities of preventing this from happening, by timely careers information. An explanation of the Service's quiescent attitude in this respect can be found in the exclusiveness of the apprenticeship system: there are definite advantages in attaining craftsman status *per se*, irrespective of skill; and while the training of apprentices for one-skill jobs may be narrow, non-apprenticed workers go, by and large, without any systematic training. There will be occasion in later chapters to enlarge upon these matters.

RECRUITMENT AND SELECTION IN THE VARIOUS INDUSTRIES

No attempt has been made in this enquiry to obtain a detailed account of the recruiting procedure of the various firms. While a few big firms have mapped out systems of recruitment and selection, the majority proceed in a less methodical manner. Firms were asked about their ways of taking on apprentices; but many do not keep records of the selection, the date of engagement, or the type of school the apprentices came from. Moreover, a small pilot enquiry had shown that some information given in interviews was of dubious accuracy.[2]

Firms have their own ways of finding apprentices. It appears that in these circumstances numbers of boys suitable for, and

---

[1] *Choice of Careers*. New Series, No. 24, p.2 and No. 64, p.4 respectively. The booklets on the printing trades are much more outspoken regarding the life-long narrow specialisation of most journeyman printers; No. 45 (New Series), for instance, states on p.27: 'Strict rules are laid down about the kind of work each group of craftsmen may do'.

[2] A firm's answer, for instance, that 90% of its apprentices had been educated at the secondary technical school was found to be hardly compatible with other information given by the firm. Another example is an apprentice's statement that the approach to his employer had been made through his headmaster, whereas in fact the father had found the employer ; only subsequently was the headmaster asked to write to the boy's prospective employer.

desirous of, apprenticeship find no openings, whereas less suitable boys are apprenticed by not so discriminating firms. The old tradition of nepotism survives in some cases—in one firm, each of the few apprentices employed was a foreman's or chargehand's son or nephew; but the information obtained does not allow an assessment to be made of the role which nepotism plays in the recruitment of apprentices.

The several industries differ significantly in the selection and recruitment of apprentices, but in some important respects they are alike.[1] Since apprenticeship involves a contract of employment for five years, all employers are aware of the special importance of finding suitable apprentices—special, that is, over and above the general importance of engaging good workers. In recruiting apprentices, employers look for qualities of personality and home background as well as for intellectual and manual ability. Indeed, whereas there is a great variety in the emphasis on ability, stress on the former qualities is almost unanimous.

The traits which a firm will want to find in all its apprentices are, first, those desired in their capacity as employees: discipline, co-operativeness and diligence; second, those desired in the future craftsmen: manual skill, machine-mindedness, and a measure of proficiency in English and mathematics; some recruits, the firm hopes, will have the making of future supervisors, by their reliability, loyalty to the firm, initiative and the gift of leadership. Firms which do not formally distinguish several grades of apprenticeship further look out among the candidates for apprenticeship for their future technicians, technologists and managers.

Engineering

Each firm selects its own apprentices, and there is great disparity in width of choice. Some employers can recruit their apprentices selectively, since the number of applications greatly exceeds that of the places they have to offer. Many boys are attracted by such new industries as aircraft manufacture and electronics; another factor is the prestige of certain firms. A

---

[1] These observations are confined to trade apprentices—for the higher grades of apprenticeship, which occur only in a few big engineering firms, see Chapter VI.

small number of employers have the pick of the bunch. The Bristol Aeroplane Company has had applications by would-be apprentices in plenty; and some medium-sized machine-making firms enjoy a good reputation for training and have, like the B.A.C., waiting lists of applicants. By contrast, other firms, including fairly large metal-goods manufacturers and small general engineering works, find it difficult to recruit suitable apprentices. As to occupations, foundry apprentices have been hard to get, the main deterrents being dirt and heat.

Pupils of the secondary technical school are much in demand as trade apprentices. A pass in the school's internal examination has been made the educational qualification for the upper of the B.A.C.'s two trade apprenticeships. Other firms welcome them as apprentices even without that examination (to the headmaster's regret). Employers are found to complain that successful pupils of the secondary technical school consider themselves above apprenticeship level and seek employment in white-collar jobs, a grievance which reflects the strong demand for pupils of the technical school.[1]

The method of selection is not standardized. Some employers use more or less elaborate tests; some go by instinct; in some firms the engagement of apprentices is left to the shop foremen.[2]

Nor does uniformity obtain in the selection for the higher-grade apprenticeship which is above craft apprenticeship but below professional level. (For this grade we use the term 'Engineering apprenticeship', following the terminology which is used in the South West—see p.88 below).

But the various schemes for Engineering apprenticeship have this in common that educational qualification is a prerequisite of selection; the most frequent standard of entry is the G.C.E. (O). Engineering apprenticeship is thus devised so as to attract grammar-school boys.

---

[1] This evidence seems worth recording, seeing that

'In general the secondary technical school has failed to fulfil the hopes that were held out for it in 1939. There has been no great expanse of technical education at the secondary level, and, what is more significant, the new schools have not as yet carved out for themselves a distinctive and essential role in the tripartite division'. (Olive Banks, *Parity and Prestige in English Secondary Education*, p.166 (1955).)

[2] See also the subsequent section Probation.

Building
Building apprentices are mostly recruited by individual firms; boys who seek the help of the youth employment office for finding an opening are referred to the secretary of the Bristol Association of Building Trade Employers who is also joint secretary of the local apprenticeship committee.

The great majority—by one informant put at over 90%—of the applicants for building apprenticeships want to be carpenters; this is quite out of proportion to the demand: of Bristol's registered apprentices in all building trades, under 40% are carpenters. Many applicants have therefore to be persuaded to take up bricklaying or plastering, or to be told that there are no other openings. For, whereas in the recruitment of carpenters supply exceeds demand, it is the other way round in the recruitment for the trowel trades, especially plastering. The unpopularity of these trades (similar to that of foundry work among engineering trades) is the reason why they were chosen for inclusion in this enquiry. Several explanations came forward of the fact that trowel work is less sought after than woodwork; (a) while carpentry is familiar to all boys, being taught in secondary modern schools, bricklaying and plastering are not; (b) the inherent skill and therefore the prestige of the trowel trades is lower than that of carpentry and of plumbing (painting comes last, both by the criterion of manual skill and by that of intelligence required); (c) there is also some awareness of the long-term threat to security of employment in the traditional trowel trades by the growing competition of new building methods and materials.

Applications for bricklayer apprenticeships still come forward from boys with a family tradition in this craft; besides, the bricklayer has better chances of promotion than most other building craftsmen: general foremen are usually chosen from among carpenters and bricklayers, as they see the whole building going up from its foundations. Plasterers, on the other hand, rarely rise to become general foremen: 'they are 99% practical'. While general building contractors have difficulties in finding plastering apprentices, the director of a firm specialising in plastering said, probably exaggerating slightly, that he has four candidates for each apprenticeship opening.

Most apprentices for the trowel trades are recruited from secondary modern schools, but there is an occasional bricklayer and even plasterer apprentice who has been in the building department of the secondary technical school. This department, just as the same school's engineering department, is held in high esteem by employers; and in building as well as in engineering, some firms appear to be able to attract a high proportion of boys from the secondary technical school as apprentices.

In the experience of the Youth Employment Officer, few applicants for building apprenticeships, not only in the trowel trades, have the ambition to become anything more than a craftsman, whereas many a recruit for an apprenticeship in engineering regards himself as a future works manager. However, among the trowel-trade apprentices interviewed by us, one or two bricklayers and plasterers were obviously determined to go ahead.

Printing

In Bristol, the printing industry stands out in having a common board for the selection of apprentices in all printing trades for all printing firms. Paulton near Norton Radstock, with the large printing and bookbinding works of Purnell & Sons, formerly in Bristol, is included in this scheme. In smaller towns (including Bath) and in rural areas, although Local Joint Industrial Committees of the Printing Industry are in being, the selection of apprentices is not centralised but is made by individual firms.

To implement the industry's National Scheme for apprenticeship, there is in Bristol a Joint Apprenticeship Committee, with joint secretaries drawn from the employers' association and from the unions respectively.

The trade unions which are concerned with apprenticeship in Bristol are those of the typographers (T.A.), the lithographic artists (S.L.A.), the lithographic printers (A.S.L.P.), the stereotypers (N.S.E. & S.) and the bookbinders. While the first four are craft unions, the bookbinders (together with the machine rulers) constitute a craft section of the mixed National Union of Printing, Bookbinding and Paper Workers. The grouping by unions does not indicate the seven or eight trades in which separate apprenticeships are available in Bristol—'the complicated trade-union organisation in the industry' has been commented upon by the British Productivity Council.[1] From the technical point of view, the significant distinction is that, whatever the process, printing is done in two stages (sometimes with further intermediate stages) and, accordingly, trades and apprenticeships fall in one of two classes: (a) type-setting or picture-engraving, etc.; (b) transferring the type or picture on to paper. The T.A. has as members both classes of craftsmen, viz. compositors and machine minders; the S.L.A. has only class (a), while the A.S.L.P. and the N.S.E. & S. have only class (b). In general, the trade determines the union to which a printing tradesman belongs, but photogravure workers may belong to one of several unions.

The Bristol Joint Apprenticeship Committee of the printing trades fulfils one important function which in other industries falls to individual firms, namely the selection of apprentices to be recruited by Bristol printing houses. First, however, some functions should be mentioned which the Committee does not undertake: the keeping of registers of apprentices is left to the several trade unions ; the observance of the apprentice ratios is controlled by the fathers of chapel in each firm; and there is no supervision of the training given in individual firms.

Since 1947 the selection of apprentices for all printing trades has been centralised in the Committee and it is largely the responsibility of the employers' representative—so much so that the examination is known as 'the master printers' examination'. It consists of papers in English and in arithmetic, a written intelligence test, a medical examination, and an interview by a panel of printing experts. Firms may sponsor prospective apprentices, but even these have to pass the examination and to be approved by the Joint Committee. Candidates for apprenticeship who are not sponsored by a firm apply directly to the Committee.

Three times a year, 17 to 20 apprenticeships can, under the

[1] '*A Review of Productivity in the Printing Industry*' (1952), p.7.

present ratios, be filled in the Bristol district. There are about 75 candidates for these openings, and all of them take the written test; of these, 50 qualify for the interview, after which perhaps 25 are recommended by the selection committee for an apprenticeship in a specified printing trade.

Some of the specific qualifications looked for in apprentices for various trades are: 'good at English', for compositors; 'good at drawing' and 'colour sense', for lithographic artists; 'interest in chemistry and/or metallurgy', for stereotypers and for photo-mechanical process workers; 'mechanically minded', for machine minders. The minding of printing machines has become akin to engineers' rather than to printers' work. Indeed, a member of the examining body remarked that the main reason why candidates for machine-minding apprenticeship were examined in English was not that they would need it in their work but that they would have to be able to take notes and to sit for examinations at the School of Printing.

Some employers appreciate the Committee's service in finding out for which of the various printing trades a boy is most suitable. One large firm, however, puts prospective apprentices through a test of its own, either before or after the examination by the Joint Apprenticeship Committee. About half of this firm's apprentices are grammar-school or technical-school boys; most of these are selected by the Committee, but if doubtful, the firm tests the candidate again, before accepting him. The other half, modern-school leavers, mostly apply to the firm direct, which tests them before sponsoring them for examination by the Committee. In spite of all this vetting, about 10% of the accepted apprentices are said to prove of such poor quality that surprise was expressed that they had passed the screening.

Now and then a printing firm leaves an apprenticeship opening vacant for several months because it is not satisfied with the available candidates, although they are recommended by the Committee. On the other hand, some of the successful examinees eventually do not enter a printing apprenticeship offered to them but take jobs in other industries. Although no numerical data could be obtained, it seems that this happens rather frequently in the case of grammar-school boys.

The wariness in the recruiting of apprentices is so great because of the strict limitation in the number of apprentices allowed to a firm and because of the demarcation which in the printing industry is rigid from the very beginning: an apprentice cannot, under existing regulations, be transferred to another printing trade for which he may come to show greater aptitude or better liking when he has started work. However, according to an informant who should know, the modern processes no longer coincide with the defined apprenticeable trades.

The selection board finds the educational attainment of the candidates for apprenticeship rather poor. Why, then, are printers very largely recruited at 15 years from secondary modern schools? The answer lies in the employers' concern with recruiting boys who are likely to be content to remain printers. 'We are not out for the brightest boys, for we want workers, not bosses,' was one explanation. A grammar-school boy was instanced who completed his printing apprenticeship and obtained his City & Guilds certificate, but who found the work not up to his capacity, became frustrated, and left the industry —a twofold loss in manpower: the printer himself and his part of the journeyman-strength which is the basis for the apprentice ratio.

On the merits of 15 as the age of entry into, and six years as the duration of, apprenticeship opinions seem to differ, both among employers and among trade unions. Some employers value an extra year of full-time education after the statutory school-leaving age, others find industrial training from 15 onward more useful. The T.A. and the bookbinders' union allow a year's full-time education until 16 to be deducted from the six-year apprenticeship period; the three other craft unions do not.

PROBATION

The probationary period preceding the indenture of a prospective apprentice is, under the present regulation of the apprenticeship system, not among the more important issues. But a short discussion of probation will throw light on certain aspects of the working of the system. The following recommendation made in 1943 by the Building Apprenticeship and Training Council may serve as the starting point of the discussion:—

'The apprenticeship agreement should provide that probation served after the age of 15 years has been attained should count as part of the period of apprenticeship, i.e. that the commencement of the period of apprenticeship should be dated back to the beginning of the period of probation. . . . A decision on suitability for apprenticeship should be given by the employer as early as possible within a maximum period of probation of six months.'[1]

The relevant points are:

1. The employer is entitled to subject the prospective apprentice to a trial period before undertaking the contractual obligation to employ and train him for five years.

2. The interests of the intending apprentice are to be protected in two ways: (a) the probation period is not to be used to prolong the apprentice's service beyond the term of indentured apprenticeship; (b) those probationers whom the employer does not accept as apprentices are to get this decision at an age at which they still have the chance of being apprenticed by another employer.

The two desiderata point to abuses on the part of some employers in the imposition of a probationary period. In addition, however, the period of probation has indirect, unintended implications which are bound up with the age limits for serving apprenticeship.

The pertinent conditions are different in each of the three industries under review which are therefore considered separately.

Printing

In Printing, apprenticeship is so neatly organised that no problems arise from the probationary period of three months which 'may precede apprenticeship in which case it is counted as part of the apprenticeship'. (National Scheme.)

The minimum age of entry is the statutory school-leaving age of 15 years, the duration 6 years, the age of completion normally 21 years—so that the whole period between the statutory

[1] B.A.T.C., *First Report*, para. 13G.

school-leaving age and the normal age of completion is occupied by apprenticeship and no extra time is left for a probation period. The period of probation is only three months; therefore, even if it ends in non-indenture, the would-be apprentice is still well under 16, the age of entry into apprenticeship in most other trades. Moreover, the elaborate selection procedure carried out by the Bristol Joint Local Apprenticeship Committee according to the scheme of the industry's Apprenticeship Authority makes a probationary period less important to employers in Printing than to those in other industries.

Engineering

Probation is not mentioned in the National Scheme for apprenticeship in the engineering and allied industries; but a probationary period—six months is the most frequent duration—is common, if not generally adopted.

The minimum age of entry into apprenticeship is 16, and for craft apprentices 16+ is also the upper age of entry.

For boys who enter a firm as apprentices at 16+, the first six months of their service are usually treated as a probation period. In the case of the boys who are accepted as apprentices the indenture is then back-dated to the beginning of their employment in the firm; but if the probation ends without the indenture being given, the boy, at least 16½ years old, will have great difficulty in finding another apprenticeship opening, because of the scarcity of openings and of the rigid upper age limit for entry into craft apprenticeship. We are unable to say how often the six-months probation period fails to lead to indenture; in some medium-sized firms we were told that this happens in about one of ten cases, but it would be rash to generalise from this information.

The majority of trade apprentices come from secondary modern schools at the age of 15 plus. Usually they are engaged on the understanding that they will be indentured when reaching the age of 16; the intervening time will be treated as their period of probation.

At the B.A.C., where selection of the most elaborate kind precedes the engagement of all apprentices, recruits for low-grade apprenticeship are selected and taken on at 15+, up to a year before they can become apprentices.[1] In at least one large firm, on the other hand, recruitment precedes selection: from among the boys who are engaged as juvenile workers when they leave school at 15, apprentices are selected only shortly before their 16th birthday.

Thus, for all boys who enter a firm at 15 plus and are indentured from their 16th to their 21st birthday, the period for which they serve the employer before they are 'freed' is in fact six years rather than the five years of their formal apprenticeship. No regulation of the period of probation could alter this situation.

The pre-apprentice year poses difficult problems for employers. At a conference on The Challenge of the Bulge, Sir Reginald Verdon Smith, chairman of the B.A.C., said:

'Closely allied to the length of apprenticeship training is the need for increased flexibility in the age of entry into apprenticeship. . . . We are . . . obliged in the case of boys leaving school at 15 to waste, or to fill in as best we can, the period prior to 16 as it is a feature of an engineering national agreement "that in no case shall the apprenticeship end before the age of 21".'[2]

Building

The clause on probation in the industry's National Scheme provides that 'as a maximum, the first six months of the apprenticeship may be treated as a probationary period . . .'.

The age regulations for apprenticeship in Building are more flexible than for apprenticeship in other industries: the term of

---

[1] The majority of B.A.C. apprentices do not leave school until they are at least 16 years old and can start their apprenticeship straight away. No probation period is imposed at the beginning of apprenticeship, but the company 'reserves the right to terminate an apprenticeship at any time [during the five years' term], should the apprentice fail to make satisfactory progress in his training or education'. (B.A.C. brochure 'Apprenticeship in the Aircraft Industry', 1956, p.17). At first sight, the claim to unilateral cancellation of apprenticeship appears to infringe the contractual obligation of an employer by whom 'each apprentice . . . is given formal Indentures of Apprenticeship' (ibid.) In fact, an engineering firm is entitled to make such a reservation, for in the engineering and allied industries the apprenticeship contract is not an indenture in the legal meaning of the word but a 'written agreement' (actually it is a printed document) without seals attached to it. As already mentioned, the term indenture is quite commonly used in a wide sense.

[2] *BACIE Journal*, December, 1957, p. 219.

five years may be served between the ages of 15 and 21. According to the National Scheme, a boy taken on at 15 ought therefore to be indentured, after six months' probation, at 15½, and the indenture should be back-dated so that his apprenticeship is completed when he is 20.

In fact, employers have been tempted to prolong the probation period because so far this period has not been subject to day release, which is so widely felt in the industry as a heavy burden. We cannot assess the proportion of building-trade apprentices who in consequence of this practice serve their employer for longer than five years; but there is evidence that a considerable number complete their apprenticeship at 20.

As in Engineering, at least one substantial building firm in our sample is in the habit of engaging more 15-year old boys than it intends to apprentice and of selecting the most suitable ones after a period of probation. However, because of the flexibility of age limits for building apprenticeship, the boys not taken as apprentices by the firm are still young enough to look for apprenticeship elsewhere.

Each industry shows a different picture of the functioning of the probation period. On the whole, probation does not today play a great part in the ordering of apprenticeship, mainly because the duration of, and age limits for, apprenticeship are so rigidly fixed. Moreover, there is a tendency for probation to be supplanted by careful selection with the help of modern testing techniques. But the question of probation may come to regain greater importance if and when the regulations on duration and age limits are relaxed—a development which is desirable on many grounds. Flexibility of the age limits may call for a strengthening of the probation regulations.

VI

PRACTICAL TRAINING
AND PRODUCTIVE WORK

IT is of the nature of apprenticeship that the costs of training are to be balanced by the apprentice's contribution to production; more than that, the employer is entitled to make a profit from the apprentice's service during the period of apprenticeship. In these circumstances, it is difficult to draw the line between the legitimate exercise of the employer's right and the use of his apprentices simply as cheap labour.

The employment of apprentices is not so cheap now as it was when they received only nominal wages and 'instruction (was) their hire'[1] Today, besides paying higher wages to apprentices (higher in proportion to the wages of both craftsmen and non-apprenticed young workers[2]), the employer also bears the cost of day release for technical education: he loses the apprentice's service one day a week, yet has to pay him wages for this day. Unlike these two items of the cost of employing apprentices, the third item, practical training, is at the discretion of the individual employer[3], and it is chiefly practical training which firms are apt to cut down in one way or another in order to maximize their profit from the apprentices' service[4].

[1] W. Paley, *Moral and Political Philosophy*. Quoted from S. and B. Webb, *Industrial Democracy*, p.454.
[2] See p. 153 below.
[3] This statement has to be qualified for the training of printing apprentices, on which the trade unions have considerable influence.
[4] See, however, Chapter VII for evasion of day-release commitments.

PRACTICAL TRAINING AND PRODUCTIVE WORK

The less the skill and experience required for the job of a craftsman, the sooner and/or more effectively can an apprentice be made to do that craftsman's job. For the training of highly skilled men a firm incurs higher costs by having to wait longer—maybe until after the apprentice is freed—for its investment in training to yield dividends. A firm can do so without loss if it can reckon upon the ex-apprentice's continuing in its employment, or upon being able, by way of give and take, to engage suitable craftsmen trained by other firms. Generous spending on apprentice training is made easier by subsidies or cost-plus contracts, and to large companies it may recommend itself on considerations of prestige, advertisement or tax advantage.

An apprentice is 'something between a hindrance and a help' to his employer; at the beginning of his term he is obviously more of a hindrance, at the end he is a help—but when does the transition take place? In our interviews, managers and foremen were asked at what stage a craft apprentice becomes remunerative to the firm. Their answers throw light on various aspects of the matter. The majority of informants said that apprentices become an asset at about 18 years of age; this reflects the importance of growing maturity as well as of two years' experience (it also explains, if an explanation is needed, the employers' concern for the deferment of their apprentices' call-up for National Service).

A minority of interviewees specified periods considerably shorter than two years, while a few stated much longer ones. These variations, however, could be related neither to types of firms and training methods nor to different trades; the question calls for further investigation.

In some answers, the main stress was on the difference between individual apprentices: one would be an asset after six months, others only after two or three years, some 'never.' Several informants distinguished between the time when an apprentice begins to pay his way and the time when he becomes an asset to the employer. In one or two firms we met an interesting difference between the replies from foremen and from higher management, the one saying that it took several years, the other, six to twelve months; some of these answers seem to be coloured by preconceived ideas on the appropriate length of apprenticeship. To sum up, as a rule the service of craft apprentices was said to become profitable to the employer well within the first half of their term.

Engineering

The general features and problems of the practical training of apprentices appear most fully in the engineering and allied industries.

Quality and methods of a firm's apprentice training depend on many factors of different weight and different conspicuousness and on their varying combination and interaction. The long list of these factors includes the size of firm and/or establishment, its main product and the diversity of its product; location (in the midst of a large labour market or isolated?)[1]; age of plant and methods of production. It would be helpful if a system of plant evaluation existed, analogous to that of job evaluation. But since no such system has been worked out, we must try to pick out the factors most important for apprenticeship and to appreciate their interaction.

The size of a firm or establishment, in terms of number of employees, is generally regarded as the main factor determining a firm's apprentice training. But this view needs qualification: the factor of size is entwined with two other factors. One of these is the class of work which is done by a given firm; precision work and work calling for the craftsman's judgment and technical grounding demand higher skill and therefore require, and afford, better apprentice training than does engineering work with not-so-close tolerances and less intricacy. Then there is the factor: length of production runs; in descending order of length of run, we find the following conditions. In mass production, fitting is replaced by assembling (as in the big motor-car plants) and comparatively few craftsmen are employed; among the firms which we interviewed, some of the largest, in terms of total employees, have a high proportion of semi-skilled workers—in one firm double the number of craftsmen—and the training of their few apprentices is indifferent. In works with long runs of production, though not by

[1] See Chapter X passim.

assembling methods, there is a great amount of specialisation of craftsmen, and the apprentice is liable to be trained for a one-skill job. Batch production, and even more so the making of prototypes and custom-built machinery, requires versatile, more highly skilled craftsmen and thus creates both the need and the opportunity for broader and fuller training.

However, the notion of different lengths of run in production is not as clear-cut as all that. From the point of view of comprehensive craftsmanship and thorough all-round apprentice training, the size of the unit of the product may blur the differences. A single huge product such as an aeroplane requires a multitude of identical components and of identical engineering operations, and in these respects gives rise to long-run, partly even to mass-production. This helps to explain why in an aircraft works semi-skilled workers may constitute a considerable part of the labour force; why many of the craftsmen in such a works are specialising in one-skill jobs, and why the training of its trade apprentices is far from all-round.

Whatever the size of an establishment, there can be few plants in which all the work is high-skill work; but great differences prevail : at the one end of the scale are firms in which a large part of the work requires precision and/or versatility; at the other end of the scale, some branches of the engineering industry seem to require very little, if any, precision work; the majority of firms are somewhere between the extremes, and the over-all quality of a firm's apprentice training will largely depend on where it stands on this scale.

Apprenticeship in different firms is affected not only by these largely technological factors but also by the kind of regime which prevails, the climate of apprenticeship, as it were.

THE CLIMATE OF APPRENTICESHIP IN VARIOUS ENGINEERING FIRMS

No two firms are alike as employers and trainers of apprentices, but three types can be distinguished, although, as would be expected, hardly any firm represents a single type unmixed.

The types which may be termed 'Apprentice Master, Traditional Style,' and, deviating from this pattern in two different directions, 'Scientific Apprentice Management', and 'Apprentice Farming' have the following characteristic features:

TYPE I. APPRENTICE MASTER, TRADITIONAL STYLE

Director (also other executives) risen from apprenticeship; autocratic; engineering intuition.

Selection of apprentices: careful; personal connection and/or handwritten application; no test, choosing 'by instinct'; boys from secondary technical school preferred.

No Grading: all start as craft apprentices; anyone can rise to become designer or manager, with or without passing examinations; executive posts reserved for firm's own employees.

Technical Courses: considered poor and/or unnecessary, but contact with college kept.

Training Schedule: drawn up but not in methodical order, nor always adhered to.

Training: subordinate to, and intermixed with, production work; emphasis on all-round training rather than on thorough training.

Supervision: watchful, by director himself; 'everybody always expected to give of his best'; regular progress reports.

No piece-rates to any worker, no shop bonuses, but overall bonus; 'good-conduct money' for apprentices.

Paternalism: against modern ideas of management.

Pace of work: drive.

Director convinced that firm's arrangement of apprenticeship could not be bettered.

The four firms in our sample which most purely represent this type range in size from 250 to 1,200 employees.

TYPE 2. SCIENTIFIC APPRENTICE MANAGEMENT

Executives: not, as a rule, self-made men. Specialisation of functions.

Recruiting: separate for various apprentice grades, based on different examinations passed at secondary schools.

Selection: elaborate. School reports, tests, inquiries into home-background and hobbies, medical examination.

Grades of apprenticeship (see above) are linked with a scaled system of crafts and higher occupations respectively.

Technical courses: considered an essential part of training; day-release until completion of apprenticeship. Category of courses (City and Guilds Certificates—National Certificates) related to grade of apprenticeship.

PRACTICAL TRAINING AND PRODUCTIVE WORK

Training Schedule: laid down and adhered to.

Special Training Shop for initial period (which differs for different apprenticeship grades) before entering shop-floor.

Training of trade apprentices: restricted in breadth; early 'specialisation'; aim: high skill and precision, appropriate to requirement of each job, in narrow field.

Supervision by special training officers; regular progress reports.

Pace of work: leisurely.

Experimenting with their apprenticeship arrangements.

The three firms of this type in our sample have respectively 800, 5,000 and 20,000 employees.

TYPE 3. APPRENTICE FARMING

Recruiting: firm has little choice; difficult to get sufficient numbers of acceptable standard; nearly all apprentices engaged at 15; complaints about recruits' low educational level.

Training Scheme: either non-existent, or only on paper.

Apprentices used as cheap labour (maybe not only in the firm's interest, but also in the foremen's).

High ratio of apprentices to craftsmen.

No higher-grade apprentices.

Technical Courses: Day-release granted not at all or grudgingly. High proportion of apprentices who do attend courses, go to Day Continuation School; no co-operation between firm and Technical College.

In large works, little supervision; no records kept; apprentices pick up the know-how or get it from older apprentices; narrow experience of machines (no ' moving on ').

In small shops, apprentices become jacks of all trades, as far as the business of the firm goes.

Five firms in the sample conform closely to this type; four of them have fewer than a hundred employees each, but the fifth has well over 500. (And there is evidence that this is not a unique case among larger firms).

GRADES OF APPRENTICESHIP

A sorting-out of apprentices by type and by degree of their capacity takes place in every establishment. Even where only one is employed, he may remain on the shopfloor or else come to take part in the management or to function as a technician (though probably only as part of his work). Bright boys are soon 'ear-marked for higher jobs,' assiduous ones work their way up.

Formal grading of apprenticeship is distinct from informal sorting-out by a rationalisation of the allocation: recruits are from the beginning of their apprenticeship assigned to the level which seems appropriate; account is taken of the increasing vertical division of labour; and the selection is based on the educational standard reached by the boys in secondary schools.

In most firms in the survey area no formal grading of apprentices takes place: all apprentices are given the same standing in the firm, viz. that of craft apprentice. From this common platform, each is left to advance—as the firm sees it, according to his capacity and application; as the apprentice sees it, also according to the amount and quality of the training he receives. The unofficial groups, by eventual attainment, into which the apprentices fall may be described in the words of one manager as:—the single-purpose man; the multi-purpose man who may be made a chargehand or foreman; and the technician (progress or planning engineer, draughtsman) or middle manager. A small proportion of apprentices rise further to become designers or other technologists, or senior managers.

In firms with such informal grading, no marked distinction of status appears to develop, at any rate not during apprenticeship.

Among the firms covered by this study which have developed an ordered hierarchy of apprenticeship, the B.A.C. alone makes use for its grading of all the different levels of the secondary-school system. It has, in ascending order, two Trade Apprenticeships, an Engineering Apprenticeship and an Undergraduate Apprenticeship.[1] Trade Apprentices for the 'A' course are recruited from secondary modern schools; for the 'B' course, the standard has been, since 1956, the passing of the examination of the secondary technical school. The educational standard for Engineering Apprenticeship is the G.C.E. (ordinary level); the majority of the B.A.C.'s Engineering Apprentices are thus recruited from grammar schools (including public schools).[2] The qualification for the Student Apprenticeship includes a pass in

[1] Formerly called Student Apprenticeship.
[2] The U.E.I. certificate is of recent development in Bristol.

86

three mathematics and science subjects at advanced level. Grading schemes of some other firms will be discussed presently.

Student Apprentices—now called Undergraduate Apprentices—at the B.A.C., and in other firms, are apprentices only in name (and in wearing the apprentices' green overalls; so that on their progression through the works they are not at first sight distinguishable from Trade and Engineering Apprentices). The youth holding a G.C.E.(A) and accepted by a university, spends in the firm a pre-university year and subsequently the university long vacations, and he draws wages during these periods. But he follows a normal university career; he becomes a qualified engineer by obtaining a university degree, not by serving an apprenticeship with the firm; and the firm pays neither wages to him during term time nor his university fees. This organisation of training is quite different from the system of sandwich courses as part of a real apprenticeship. Rather is it the kind of arrangement made for the gaining of practical experience by a student for the Social Science Diploma. Although the Undergraduate Apprenticeship is called an apprenticeship, the attachment is not binding: Undergraduate Apprentices are not indentured. Nor are they expected to contribute to production during their stay in the various departments; the wages they receive are more of the nature of retaining fees, to secure their allegiance to the firm after their graduation. Whether or not this policy on the part of a firm is successful—and we have met Undergraduate Apprentices who were considerably disillusioned—Undergraduate Apprenticeship does not entail the problem intrinsic to genuine apprenticeship of a conflict between the requirements of production and of training; the term Undergraduate Apprentice is thus a misnomer, and these young men should not be included in the number of real apprentices. This applies also to 'Graduate Apprentices'.

It may clear the issue to devote a paragraph or two to the discussion of the names given to various apprenticeship grades. Grading of apprenticeship is mostly done by individual firms and is still in an experimental stage. It is therefore natural, but none the less confusing, that a given grade is found to be described by different terms, and that a given term may denote different grades. 'Trade' and 'Craft' appear to have become synonymous beyond redress; the B.A.C.'s A and B courses, for example, one without, the other with specific educational qualification for entry, are both 'Trade' courses and both promise a 'skilled craftsman's' career, the latter course with possibilities of further rise. The terms trade and craft apprenticeship, just as the terms tradesman and craftsman (and also journeyman) are accordingly used as synonyms in this study.

The term Engineering apprenticeship was used in *Apprenticeship 1925-26* (p. 88) and has come to be accepted in the South West (and throughout the British aircraft industry) for the grade of apprenticeship which aims at producing technicians and junior managers; elsewhere, the same grade can be found to be styled as Technical apprenticeship[1] or, more confusingly, as Student apprenticeship. In view of this use of the term Student apprenticeship, it is not unwelcome that the aircraft industry has dropped the term in favour of Undergraduate apprenticeship. However, since it is our submission that the relation between a university student and his intermittent employer is not a true apprenticeship either in letter or in spirit, 'Undergraduate apprenticeship' is excluded from this study.

Other firms have adopted, or are experimenting with, schemes resembling that of the B.A.C., but less finely graded. The present scheme of the Westinghouse Brake & Signal Co. consists of one Trade apprenticeship grade, an Engineering apprenticeship and a Student apprenticeship;[2] and the same categories feature in the grading scheme of E.M.I. Engineering Development, Wells. Douglas (Kingswood) have a Works apprenticeship, a Craft apprenticeship and a Pupil apprenticeship; and Parnalls, Fishponds, a Craft apprenticeship and an Engineering apprenticeship. In nearly all firms where apprenticeship grading has been introduced, the various occupations for which apprentices are trained are allocated to an appropriate grade—the traditional trades to one of the Trade, Craft or Works apprenticeships; planning and progress engineers, etc., to the Engineering or Pupil apprenticeships; draughtsmen apprenticeship is sometimes in a class by itself, sometimes part of one or other of the grades mentioned.

---

[1] The Carr Report uses the apt description " Technician Apprentices."
[2] Equivalent to Undergraduate apprenticeship at the B.A.C.

PRACTICAL TRAINING AND PRODUCTIVE WORK

The practical training of a firm's apprentices of various grades is different, and so is their technical education.[1] Furthermore, there is a marked inequality between the standing in the firm of Trade apprentices and of Engineering apprentices respectively. We asked several persons who seemed unbiased which gap was wider: that between Trade apprentices and semi-skilled youths, or that between Engineering apprentices and Trade apprentices; each time an answer was given, it was that the second gap was greater. More light will be thrown on this matter in the next chapter.

CONDITIONS IN VARIOUS FIRMS

We now turn to a review of the apprenticeship conditions prevailing in various firms. It seems useful here to refer for comparison to the specimen Syllabuses of Training which the National Joint Body of the engineering industry approved after the last war.

The existing five specimen syllabuses (for apprentice fitters and turners; moulders and core-makers; pattern makers; sheet-metal workers) are drawn up on a uniform pattern with identical phrasing for certain general recommendations.

The Syllabuses emphasise the desirability of preliminary training, of systematic training and of all-round training.

'Preliminary training should be arranged to give the boy an insight into the processes carried out in Engineering Works and the reasons why these processes are carried out. In a large Works this should preferably be done in an Apprentice Workshop by an instructor or in a section of the Factory devoted exclusively to the training of boys in the charge of an Apprentice Instructor or some other competent person. In smaller Works this arrangement might not be practicable, but in any case it should be the duty of some specified person to give guidance and preliminary training to new entrants.'

Each Syllabus gives an Outline of Practical Instruction in the works during the whole of the apprenticeship period; the processes to be learnt are specified, together with the

---

[1] See p. 95 and Chapter VII *passim.*

length of time to be devoted to each; progress from simple jobs to more difficult and responsible ones is urged.

The Outlines provide for a considerable breadth of training. 'It is considered that either a skilled fitter or skilled turner requires a basic grounding in the other's trade. Since a boy normally does not know which trade he desires to follow until he has gained some experience of the work for himself, apprentices should be engaged as "fitters and turners" to start with, but should specialise in one trade or the other after they have received general training in the basic processes both at the bench and in the Machine Shop.' However, the wording of the general recommendation (in all the Syllabuses) that 'an all-round training should be given as far as possible' is still not incompatible with the evasive clauses in the National Scheme for apprenticeship in the engineering industry:

'Arrangements, as far as practicable, shall be made for an apprentice to receive a measure of training in those trades which are closely related to the one he is learning.

'Arrangements, as far as practicable, shall be made to exchange apprentices between works and, where the firm is large enough, between departments in order to give them wider and more varied experience.'

In the Syllabuses, the recommendations for training in large firms are modified for smaller firms, and the following examination of training conditions in various firms is in the first place based on this distinction.

How, then, does training in different engineering firms compare with the standard set up in the Specimen Syllabuses? The answer is not merely that, as one would expect, performance falls short of the model, but also that that the training principles of the syllabuses are not altogether best observed in large firms; in some respects, the syllabuses provide for out-dated conditions.

In principle, there are two different methods of practical training:—

(a) The traditional method. The apprentice starts straight away on the shop floor, picks up the know-how, moving on from one machine, operation, process, craftsman to another, as the flow of the firm's orders dictates. Production requirements (and the foremen's and craftsmen's consideration of their earnings) also determine what instruction the apprentice receives, how much, and when.

(b) The modern method. Basic training is separated from production: apprentices spend an initial period in a special training shop under an instructor, learning to do certain basic operations by hand, and then to work on machines; when they go on to the shop floor they are put to production work, with varying degrees of supervision and of opportunity of gaining experience.

Between these types there are two intermediate methods of practical training; the apprentice may start on the shopfloor but, instead of being attached to a craftsman, he is put under the immediate direction of the foreman or of a chargehand; and, one step further, a corner of the workshop may be set apart for training under a picked craftsman as apprentice instructor. In the following discussion, unless otherwise stated, the former is included with method (a), the latter with method (b).

(a) In most of the firms we visited, training takes place on the shopfloor; apprentices join from the start the routine manufacture in the shops. In some firms—by no means only small ones—the apprentice is still attached to one craftsman at a time; the knowledge of the trade is thus passed on from one generation of craftsmen to the next, while they work. This implies that instruction is given as and when production demands or allows, and also according to the capacity and willingness to teach and to the temperament of the teacher-craftsman. However, the trend seems to be for apprentices to be made the direct responsibility of a supervisor, (foreman or chargehand).[1] Under either arrangement, the task on which the apprentice is employed depends mainly on the current output requirements of the firm or the department. More often than not, he is treated first and foremost as a worker; training is subordinate to production; and methodical sequence in his training is absent.

Within this unsystematic set-up there is however a wide range in the care and thoughtfulness of instruction: some craftsmen

---

[1] Fitting is an exception: in firms where other apprentices are now put to work by supervisors, the apprentice fitter is usually still attached to an adult fitter.

and foremen are real mentors to the apprentices whom they are training and use the method 'which is not sufficiently often emphasised, of explanation, demonstration, imitation and repetition'.[1] But this is frequently not found practicable in prevailing conditions: in a busy workshop apprentices may spend their time watching the craftsmen at work, without having the opportunity of practising under supervision. Further, the craftsmen to whom apprentices are attached may be chosen not so much for their skill as for their fatherly interest. Last, but not least, the total period of such attachment to craftsmen for training may be of short duration; in many cases the apprentice, having learnt to operate a given machine, is left to operate it, as a productive worker and without further training, for months on end. Much the same differences prevail where the apprentice's training is the direct responsibility of the foreman: the quality of training ranges from personal instruction and supervision to leaving the apprentice to pick up knowledge as best he can, sometimes from other apprentices little older than himself.

The apprentices' progression within a workshop is largely decided by the foreman; their progression from shop to shop is decided by higher management.

Quite a few firms have training schedules for apprentices in various trades, with specified periods during which apprentices are to stay in each shop or department. Records are kept, often in diagrammatic form, of each apprentice's progress, and in some firms the foreman of each department reports on the apprentices' conduct and proficiency when they move on. Such records exist even in some quite small firms whose training may in fact be far from adequate.

A firm's having a training schedule does not imply that its apprentices get to know the various departments in a fixed order. Some firms plot each apprentice's movements in advance for the whole five years of his apprenticeship, but the order in which the departments follow each other differs between the curriculum of one fitter and that of another fitter, etc. The firm's purpose is to make the best use of working space and of

[1] H. C. Haslegrave, 'Craft Training and Certification', p.13. A.T.I. Paper, 1948.

teaching facilities; also, to distribute the apprentices' contribution to production evenly among departments. 'They go to the section where we can fit them in' is a typical statement; the manager who made it was quite confident that the order in which apprentices move through the departments is inessential for successful training. This view is not shared by all apprentices: many are dissatisfied with the order in which they are moved, as impeding the understanding of their craft.

Moreover, training schedules may be laid down but not implemented. Training plans often give way to the pressure of output: an apprentice is kept in a busy department long beyond the scheduled period and used for productive work on the machine on which he has become proficient. Conversely, he may have a very short spell in, and get only perfunctory experience of, a department where business at the time is slack.

So far, we have treated training on the shopfloor as a single method of training; in fact, the method assumes one form in some of the smallest firms (under 50 employees, say) and two other forms in firms of medium to large size. In a small general engineering shop, an apprentice is moved on from one machine to another by the very requirements of the firm's work. The danger is not that he is moved on too little, but on the contrary that, within the compass of his employer's products and equipment, he becomes a jack of all trades. Lack of thoroughness and acquaintance with only a narrow range of often antiquated machines are the charges which trade unions, large firms and technical colleges level against the small shops' training; however, the apprentices themselves are usually not troubled by these shortcomings: they feel that they have the freedom of their employer's shop and learn all there is to learn in the business. This does not mean that these apprentices are right in their judgment, but their contentment is in telling contrast to the dissatisfaction felt by many trade apprentices in larger firms.

In the not-so-small firm with a number of shops or departments the organisation of work is not naturally conducive to breadth of training. With increasing specialisation of both men and machines, many firms' demand for skilled labour is largely for one-skill men. Unless the management arranges for, and insists on, the movement of apprentices, these are liable to be kept in one shop throughout their service and/or in one repetitive job for long periods. The denial of broader training and varied experience is a sore point with eager apprentices and the cause of wide-spread frustration. In some firms, the criticism goes, only boys who prod and clamour are moved on; sometimes the shop steward helps them, although he has no official say in the matter; in other cases it is said that an apprentice has to make a nuisance of himself with the charge-hand in order to be moved. When we asked directors and managers about their training schedules, quite a few stated readily that apprentices usually had to ask before they were moved on, or even that they stayed in the shop in which they started. It is in this sort of firm (which may have hundreds of employees) that apprentice training is liable to be at its worst: apprentices are given neither a systematic basic training nor the opportunity of varied experience through 'moving on.'

Yet there are other firms of medium or large size which also adhere to the traditional method of training on the shopfloor but whose training is of a different order. Firms whose work does not consist mainly in long-run production require and train men of more than one-job skill. Although no extra personnel, factory space or equipment is devoted to training, apprentices receive a fair amount of instruction on the shop-floor, and training schedules are in operation by which apprentices are moved from one shop or section to another about every six months during the whole or most of their five years of service. They work, however, in semi-skilled departments, such as assembling shops, as well as in skilled ones.

While this sort of training produces versatility (the trade entered in the indentures is quite often 'general engineering'), it tends to be wanting in thoroughness. Lack of careful and expert instruction is a major grievance of apprentices in firms where they are trained or 'exposed to training' on the shopfloor. A few informants, it is true, argued that there were merits in the trial-and-error method of learning; a works manager, looking back to his own apprenticeship, considered it an advantage that he had to pick up much of the know-how, and one or two apprentices qualified their complaints by remarking

94

that one learns quite a lot by one's mistakes. Even so, one would think that not-so-bright boys would learn little by the teach-yourself method, and that even bright ones would benefit if, at least at one stage, their training were systematic and informed by the best available technique.

(b) The second method of conducting apprenticeship, the separation of training from output, has been adopted by some of the larger firms in the survey area. We found special apprentice training shops in five of the eleven works with 500 or more employees which we interviewed[1] (in addition, one firm with fewer employees, in a small town, puts its apprentices for two months in a training shop in which non-skilled workers are trained for one-skill jobs).

In these firms the apprentice does not start his service on the shopfloor, but in the special shop, for basic training; this initial period, ranging from three to twelve months, varies between firms and between trades.

After what has been said above on the deficiencies of training as an adjunct of production, the removal of training from the shopfloor has obvious advantages: scientific training methods, based on time and motion study and covering recent techniques, are more successful than the traditional method of letting apprentices learn the often indifferent skill of the present generation of craftsmen; if training is set apart and made the full-time responsibility of skilled and experienced instructors, it can proceed systematically instead of being subordinated to the exigencies of production; the pace of training is freed from the pressure of speed which is kept up on the shopfloor for the sake of profit, bonuses and piece-rate earnings.

The firms with special training workshops usually have apprentice-grading systems—they represent the Scientific Apprentice Management type. The training of their apprentices is rationalized: content and duration of each apprentice's training are determined by the occupation in which the firm intends to employ him. (The term training stands here for actual training as distinct from the uniform five-year period of apprenticeship). The Engineering apprentice gets all-round training to a considerable degree, including experience in the

---

[1] These five do not include all firms with over 1,000 employees.

drawing office, in addition to technical education leading to the O.N.C. The craft apprentice of higher grade will spend a year in the training workshop and after this basic training undergo a period of 'formative training' in a number of departments. Thereafter, he specializes—in one large firm fitters, for example, specialize in one of four fitting trades. The lower level of craft apprenticeship is characterised by much earlier sub-specialisation. No specification is laid down of what constitutes a trade; in the case of the many one-skill jobs, the 'trade' is narrow, and the training for it is correspondingly narrow; an example is the already mentioned training of apprentice machinists in one branch of machining only. The apprentice in this category leaves the training workshop after a few months; he may then get a period of 'touring' round the works before he joins the shop in which he is to remain and specializes; the greater part of his five years of service is spent on routine production.

However, during these later years the apprentice remains under the supervision of the training officer's staff as well as under that of the foreman, and he will be made to become really skilled in his specialised job. Furthermore, firms with scientific apprentice management set high store by technical education, and their apprentices of all grades continue to attend technical courses during working hours up to the end of their term.

It must be kept in mind that apprentice training varies from firm to firm; and it seems apposite to repeat that, while most firms show more features characteristic of one type of apprenticeship regime than of the other types, few firms are pure specimens.

In firms with scientific apprentice management, craft apprentices rarely complain about the quality of their basic training; but complaints about early and narrow specialisation are frequent. This grievance indicates a serious problem. It is of the nature of grading that the more skilful and varied work which requires fuller training is allocated to apprentices of higher grades, and that lower-grade apprentices are left with the simpler, more repetitive work for which much less training is needed. From the firm's point of view it would be a waste to train low-grade apprentices for more than one-skill jobs, but the expectations of many boys are disappointed by the limitation of their training.

The ensuing *ennui* of low-grade apprentices is intensified, it would seem, in firms where sharp vertical division of labour goes together with pronounced distinction of status according to social background and type of secondary education. Evidence of this emerged from conversations with apprentices and other informants from various parts of the country.

In pointing out that in certain respects the traditional method as applied in training-conscious firms appears to be superior to the modern method of apprentice training, we are far from suggesting that the former is the right method. On the contrary, the future lies obviously with 'scientific apprentice management'. It is for this very reason that the shortcomings of this method of training should be clearly seen; only when the ills are diagnosed, can consideration be given to remedial measures.

An innovation in the organisation of apprentice training which is now being recommended is the introduction of Group Apprenticeship Schemes. The idea is explained in the Carr Report (para. 39):

'Inability to give the whole range of training required is a difficulty encountered by the smaller firms and by those larger firms which employ only a few persons in apprentice-trained occupations. . . . Under such a scheme a boy is apprenticed to one firm but undertakes those parts of this training which his own firm is unable to give him with other firms in the group. . . . One great advantage of a group apprenticeship scheme is that it increases the facilities for training without the need for any additional capital expenditure.'

Efforts to promote group training schemes, which have been made since 1949, are described by Professor Gertrude Williams.[1] So far, it is mainly in Engineering that these attempts have been made, and progress has been very slow. One can think of several possible reasons for this, apart from the novelty of the idea.

[1] *Recruitment to Skilled Trades*, p.132ff (1957).

First, employers may be unwilling to renounce the traditional exclusive attachment of apprentices to their firm—indentures still contain a clause forbidding the apprentice to reveal the secrets of his employer's business; however, in the light of our interviews this consideration does not seem to be a major factor in employers' lack of enthusiasm for joining group training schemes. Second, the fees payable by employers for each apprentice they have in a scheme are not inconsiderable, and this may contribute to deterring small firms from participation in a scheme. But the decisive reason why group training schemes have not caught on would appear to derive from the dual nature of apprenticeship which involves a conflict between the interests of training and of output; in the many de-skilled crafts actual training occupies only a fraction of the period of apprenticeship, and for most of their five years of service apprentices are employed in routine production. Any additional training, such as envisaged in the group training schemes, would in the firms' view be an over-training for the jobs—often one-skill jobs— which the apprentices are intended to do, and would reduce the time during which the apprentices can be profitably used as workers on production. It seems, therefore, that voluntary group apprenticeship schemes cannot be expected to make a great contribution towards improving the training for industry.

Printing[1]

There are no special training workshops in printing firms, anyhow not in the Bristol region: training is done on the shop-floor. The methods of attaching apprentices to journeymen (i.e. craftsmen) and of putting them under the immediate direction of the overseer (i.e. foreman) are intermixed.

There are two stages of printing :

(a) COMPOSING-ROOM CRAFTS

The apprentice compositor is kept for at least two years on hand composing and its ancillaries such as re-sorting the fount ('Diss') and clearing off. No non-skilled workers are admitted to the

---

[1] This section does not deal with all the different printing trades to be found in Bristol; it concentrates on the composing room crafts (setting the type) and some of the machine room crafts (printing the type).—See chapter X for printing apprenticeship in rural areas.

composing room (whereas machine minders have mates); and apprentice compositors are employed, for part of their time at least, on such jobs as breaking up type and helping the journeymen in general. Far the greatest part of composing is today done on line-setting machines, Linotype or Intertype, or on Monotype machines; keyboard operation on these machines is not very difficult, but apprentices are not allowed to learn this before the second half of their period of service. The argument for this rule is that they must first have mastered all the traditional hand compositor's tasks, ancillary as well as layout and display work. In larger firms, this 'copy preparation' is usually done by a specialist, a superior craftsmen, whereas journeymen specialise on a lower level: as keyboard operators or in one of the accessory operations, as a 'make-up hand' or a 'stone-hand', etc. A re-sorting of type is required with neither machine. The prolonged training in hand composing is nevertheless still laid down for all apprentice compositors in the Memorandum 'Workshop Training of Apprentices' by the Joint Industrial Council for the Printing and Allied Trades, 1954 Edition, and it would seem therefore, under modern conditions, to deserve the verdict of over-training. Evidence of opposite shortcomings of training will be discussed presently.

The Monotype composing method of printing is hedged in by special regulations as to training and demarcation. In this process, keyboard operation and type casting are not combined as they are in the Linotype machine but are done by two separate machines. The apprentice compositor is allowed to learn the operation of the Monotype keyboard only in his fourth year[1].

There is also a special apprenticeship in Monotype casting; while no Monotype-caster apprentice or journeyman is allowed to do any printing work other than on this machine, a compositor is allowed to work the Monotype caster as well as the various kinds of keyboard, although in fact 'it is rare for a craftsman who has become proficient in using the one type of machine to change to the other'.[2]

Training in Monotype machine operation is an exception in

---

[1] About this and some other points, e.g. the employment of a non-printer as a proof-reader, local tugs of war are carried on in spite of national agreements.

[2] 'Printing: Composing Room Crafts'. *Choice of Careers*, New Series No. 46 p.14.

that it is not given on the shopfloor; in Bristol, instruction in keyboard and in caster operation respectively was until 1956 given in a special 'school' conducted by the Monotype Corporation. Firms in S.W. England having installed Monotype machines have sent both journeymen and apprentices to this school, either for some weeks' full-time courses or for day-release courses. Since the autumn of 1956, Monotype courses are held, by the same special instructors as heretofore, in the Printing School (College of Technology) which has now moved to more spacious and better equipped premises.

The operation of the Monotype caster is indistinguishable from an engineer's job; the worker uses an engineering micrometer, is in charge of a complicated machine, and requires some knowledge of metallurgy. Of the art of printing, on the other hand, his job requires little.

(b) MACHINE-ROOM CRAFTS

The craftsmen printing the type are called machine minders. There are letterpress machine minders, lithographic machine minders, photogravure machine minders, and under the present demarcation rules, there is a separate apprenticeship in each of these trades.

A machine-minder apprentice may for a few months be attached to a journeyman to learn by watching him, and then be put to work by the overseer on a small press by himself. The rules forbid the operation of large machines by apprentices, but some apprentices are operating big machines and there is continual local strife about this between employers and unions.

The minder of a printing machine (for which he may have a non-craft worker as an assistant) 'must be sufficiently of a mechanic to understand the many adjustments of his complex machines'.[1] The skill of the machine minder is in the 'make-ready': to see that the impression of his machine is neither too heavy nor too light and to regulate the flow of ink. This job has been made simpler by the improvement of machines, of paper and of inks, and there is a wide consensus of opinion that three to four years would be long enough for this apprenticeship. The skill of making-ready might be likened to the manipulative

---

[1] 'Printing, *Choice of Careers*, New Series No. 45 p.11.

dexterity and mental concentration which are required in various processes of boot and shoe manufacture. In this industry, operatives, not apprentice-trained craftsmen, cope with similar variations and close tolerances 'in covering . . . infinitely varied lasts with a material which itself is little less variable'.[1]

The quality of training varies considerably between printing firms. The overtraining of apprentices in some firms has already been mentioned—overtraining, that is, if the conditions in large modern printing houses are taken into consideration, viz. far-reaching mechanisation and the breaking down of crafts into various narrowly specialised jobs.

Some printing firms disregard the Joint Industrial Council's recommendations for the training of apprentices and, just like many engineering firms, train one-skill men. In Printing, just as in Engineering, apprentices were found to complain that their training is sacrificed to considerations of maximum output (no set training scheme, no thorough basic training, no moving on) and that they are being used as cheap labour. Knowledgeable observers confirm that training is liable to be narrow in large firms, whereas in smaller ones the equipment is liable to be outdated and of little variety. The trade unions maintain that small establishments are better training grounds than large ones, and by way of regressive ratios, a firm which employs few journeymen has a proportionately high 'apprentice entitlement'. In one important respect, the unions' own policy makes training in small printing shops superior: the demarcation rules, which spell narrow training are, and indeed must be, relaxed where only a few printers are at work.

Many informants—mostly representing the employers' side, but also a number of apprentices—are confident that between two and four years would suffice for apprenticeship in machine-minding instead of the five to six years laid down. That in the latter years of this long period of service apprentices are used as cheap labour is the opinion voiced not only by apprentices. The training of compositors, on the other hand, is held to require five years at least; but as argued above, there are reasons

---

[1] J. H. Britton, 'Development of Machine Production in the Shoe Industry', in *Journal of the Institution of Production Engineers*, January, 1955, p.30.

to believe that the present schedule for the training of compositors is antiquated in its emphasis on hand composing; an emphasis which is mainly due to the trade unions' partiality for small firms.

Building
Despite the growing competition by modern building methods, bricklaying is still one of the major building crafts; bricklayers are employed in new construction and in repair work, by large contractors and by small jobbing firms. Plastering, with a craft force about one-quarter the size of that of bricklaying, is to some extent a special branch of the building industry: half of the country's plastereres are employed by firms specialising in this work. They undertake plastering jobs as sub-contractors to general builders. Larger general building firms may sub-contract part of the plastering yet also employ some plasterers and a few plasterer apprentices themselves; these may execute the more elaborate plastering that comes the firm's way, such as the ornamental plastering work in Bristol's new Council House.

Building operations in bricklaying and plastering are less mechanised than factory work. The trowel trades require less theoretical and mathematical knowledge and less accuracy but more manual and brachial touch and more experience of the raw materials than many engineering trades. But even though machines have not replaced trowel work by hand, there are other developments which have de-skilled these crafts. Plainness of style, simplification and uniformity of buildings have replaced ornamentality, intricacy and individual design. Standardisation and large-scale building have led to sub-specialisation within the bricklayer's and plasterer's trades, in both senses of the term specialisation: the more difficult parts of a job are done, not by the rank and file of craftsmen, but by a few of superior skill; and the trades are subdivided, so that, for instance, bricklayers specialize in work on ground floors and upper floors of council houses respectively, and that solid plastering and fibrous plastering are done by different tradesmen.

Another specific feature of the building industry with a bearing on apprentice training is the smallness of the working unit. The average size of building firms is small. And in a large firm, the labour force is split up: each building site is a unit of its own, under a separate general foreman; moreover, the apprentices on each site belong to several strictly demarcated trades. The distance of a firm's various building sites from its head office makes contact between higher managerial staff and apprentices more difficult in building firms than in factories with the same number of employees. This lack of contact was commented upon by apprentices and by foremen. One big firm endeavours to amend this, apparently with some success, by having several senior managers acting as 'apprentice masters' for the firm's apprentices in the various trades. In some other firms, the liaison is differently organised. The general foreman on each major building site bears a heavy all-round responsibility. Our impression is that apprentice training is improved where this burden is somewhat relieved. We found this to be done in one or two medium-sized firms where each building site is made the special concern of one of the directors and where technicians based on the head office do the day-to-day checking of the work on the sites.

All-round training in a building trade does not depend on deliberate moving-on, in the way it does in engineering; the completion of a building contract involves moving the apprentice to another site as a matter of course. Therefore, *ceteris paribus*, the smaller the contract—and assumedly, the smaller the firm—the more frequent the moving. Apprentices employed on large building sites have indeed complained about lack of variety of their work and training. While the basic work of building craftsmen is not so differentiated, the set of circumstances is never the same on two sites.

Practical training in the trowel trades is in Bristol almost invariably done 'on the job', by working craftsmen: in bricklaying the apprentice is attached to one man at a time; in plastering, to the team of two craftsmen and the labourer who 'gauges' the mix of plaster for them.

At 18, if not earlier, most apprentices do a man's job. That the present five-year period is unnecessarily long for apprenticeship in the trowel trades is generally agreed upon. Even a trade-union personality whom we consulted considers that four years would be sufficient. Other informants would reduce the term to three years, especially for apprentices starting at a more mature age than 15; for plastering, three years is considered fully long enough by most informants.

The great majority of interviewees confirmed, by censure or by admission, that the quality of apprentice training was poor; if the verdict was not quite so emphatic regarding plastering as regarding bricklaying, the reason may be that the plasterer's training is expected to be 'less broad' than the bricklayer's. The blame is chiefly placed on the tradesmen: bonus schemes, which are operated in Bristol fairly generally, are said to spoil not only the craftsmen's own workmanship but also the training of the next generation. Most tradesmen have 'no inclination' or 'no time' to train apprentices, or even show 'hostility' against them; foremen therefore have to endeavour to find some men who are 'tolerant of', and 'don't mind', training apprentices. 'This is a bonus firm and apprentices must do their bit', stated a plasterer; the men's over-riding concern with the pay-packet was, in another context, confirmed by an unprejudiced informant. One firm, in order to discourage slapdash work by apprentices, does not extend to them the men's bonus scheme; but on one site at least, the apprentices demonstrated against being made to do the most awkward jobs (their usual lot) when they were even denied bonus payments.

While there can be little doubt that bonus payments are a cause of the poor training which apprentices receive from building craftsmen, it would be rash to conclude without further investigation that they are the only or even the predominant cause. More knowledge is wanted particularly on the following points: is apprentice training on the job better in areas where bonus schemes have been less widely adopted than in the Bristol district[1], and how far is the tradesmen's apparent unwillingness to teach apprentices in reality an inability to teach, considering that many of those who are employed as craftsmen have themselves not gone through apprenticeship? Our enquiry produced some evidence which suggests on the one hand that a bonus scheme can be devised

[1] In the country as a whole, 'such schemes seem to have been introduced on fewer than a third of the building sites'. *The Times*, 17th December, 1956.

so as to make it advantageous for craftsmen to teach apprentices well, and on the other hand, that a non-bonus firm may prefer to attach apprentices for initial basic training to working foremen rather than to craftsmen. In both cases, apprentices find the majority of the craftsmen quite helpful and 'willing to show how things go'.

But these firms are exceptions from the rule. Insufficient teaching by craftsmen is a general source of serious dissatisfaction; other recurrent complaints are, from apprentice bricklayers, that they are employed on jobbing work only and get too little experience of construction; from apprentice plasterers, that they are kept too long on awkward jobs like that of patching up walls after the plumbing is done.

In the building firms which we visited no charges were laid, either by management or by apprentices, against the foremen. This is in marked contrast to grievances we met in engineering firms, although bonuses play their part in the earnings of foremen in both industries. The difference might be explained by the fact that in building—whether in the nature of the work or merely in continuance of long custom—it is usual for apprentices to be attached to craftsmen rather than to be under the immediate direction of the foremen. Nevertheless, in the words of a bricklayer apprentice well satisfied with his training, 'it all depends on the general foreman and the bricklayer foreman.' It seems indeed that for most trowel-trade apprentices in Bristol, the site rather than the firm is the decisive unit.

Apprentice training for the building trades meets with formidable obstacles also in other countries. 'In the custom trades, particularly building', writes an American professor of industrial education[1] 'the apprenticeship programs are confronted with serious difficulties'. Indeed, he concludes the discussion of the major relevant problems[2] with the statement that in the U.S.A. 'genuine apprenticeship has almost disappeared in the building trades'.

[1] Arthur B. Mays, *Essentials of Industrial Education*, p.64 (1952).

[2] These are: rapid changes in building methods, materials and design; seasonal fluctuations; uncomfortable working conditions; reluctance of contractors to employ apprentices; and the inherent difficulty of teaching boys on a construction job.

However, information received from other sources indicates that this statement is not of unqualified validity: in the United States, too, strong efforts are being made to make apprenticeship the only entry into the building crafts and certain other skilled occupations.

In this country, an important experiment in the training of building apprentices was made as an emergency measure after the last war, viz. the operation of the Apprentice Master Scheme. The purpose of the scheme was intensive initial training, and 'its principle [was] that groups of apprentices erect[ed] suitable buildings (mainly houses in fact) for Local Authorities under the guidance of craftsmen instructors employed by an Apprentice Master nominated by a Joint Apprenticeship Committee of the Industry. Costs in excess of a normal cost . . . [were] paid by the Ministry [of Works.]'[1] The scheme was brought to a close in 1952 owing to the need for economy; during the seven years of its existence 7,500 boys had been engaged on it.

We have no direct information on the Apprentice Master Scheme, since none of the 117 local authorities who operated it is in our survey area. The Reports of the Building Apprenticeship and Training Council, who formulated the Scheme, tell a fascinating story. (Most of the following quotations are from the Final Report).

'The scheme is regarded as having been a most admirable means of training apprentices, giving them a sound insight into craft requirements and producing excellent workers with reliability and breadth of outlook.'

The B.A.T.C. recommends that the scheme should be revived:

'Firms . . . unable to play their full part in the training of apprentices would contribute to the cost of training facilities on the lines of the apprentice master scheme . . . [which] might thus become a permanent feature of the industry.'

The financial side of this recommendation for the building industry, without reference to the method of training, was taken up in the Carr Report. In para. 43, under the heading 'Large Firms', it says:

[1] B.A.T.C., Third Report, para.86.

PRACTICAL TRAINING AND PRODUCTIVE WORK

'The principle of a contribution towards training by those firms which are themselves unable to train is one that other industries also should consider.'

Both the success of the Apprentice Master Scheme and its cost teach lessons for apprentice training in general. The success was partly due to particular circumstances, partly to features of general application: (1) 'All this work, carried out by the apprentices themselves, under the careful guidance of experienced and chosen craftsmen, became a thrilling adventure'; (2) priority in admission to the scheme was given to boys who had completed building courses in secondary technical schools, and, as mentioned before, pupils of this type of school are greatly valued by many employers of apprentices; (3) 'many boys have remained with Apprentice Masters for considerably longer periods than [the six months originally] envisaged'.

The fact that the Scheme could not be operated without subsidies draws attention to the cost of training;[1] it should be noted, however, that the scheme did not have the advantage, enjoyed by ordinary employers, of retaining the apprentices' services, at apprentices' wage rates, for several years after 'the unremunerative early period of apprenticeship.'

The observations on the Apprentice Master Scheme in the building industry lead to a reflection on modern apprentice training in general which seems to be a fitting conclusion of this chapter.

We have endeavoured to show how the dual nature of apprenticeship makes itself felt in day-to-day working life, as a conflict between the claims of learning and of serving (from the apprentice's point of view), of training and of production (from the employer's point of view). We have reviewed the admixture of the two elements in widely different proportions, ranging from the apprentice-farming type of firm where very little training is added to a great proportion of productive work, to the sandwich-course scheme under which Engineering apprentices spend half their working time on technical education, in addition to any training they received during their practical work.

[1] The cost of the whole project was about £2 million (*History of the Second World War: Manpower*, by H. M. D. Parker, p.365, 1957).

As regards the training of craft apprentices, the following facts emerge:

In modern conditions, the time needed to train apprentices in the requisite specific skills is greatly reduced, for two reasons: first, the specific skill required for many traditional trades has diminished and narrowed; second, modern training methods make it possible for a given skill to be imparted more quickly.

The requisite degree of literacy and of general education has risen—employers expect the secondary schools to look after this.

Technical education (with which the following chapter deals) is becoming increasingly necessary; it is catered for by technical colleges; the employers' contribution is to give their apprentices day release for attendance of these courses.

One attribute of apprentice training, however, seems to have fallen by the wayside. The protracted training of former times, when 'the dexterity of hand, indeed, even in common trades, [could] not be acquired without much practice and experience',[1] yielded as a by-product the habit of taking pains over a job. This by-product has ceased to be produced. The painstaking habit is part of good workmanship, in less-skilled jobs as well as in skilled ones. But the cultivation of working habits takes years and cannot be achieved within the short period, measured in months, in which so many craft apprentices today are made to acquire the specific skill which is needed for their job. All too little is being done to make up for the fact that in modern conditions the learning of specific skill does not implicitly generate 'the strenuous and business-like application to the matter in hand' which a hundred years ago was 'found in the best English workmen, and [was] their most valuable quality'.[2]

---

[1] Adam Smith, *Wealth of Nations*, Book I, Chap. X, Part II.

[2] J. S. Mill, *Principles of Political Economy*, Book I, Chapter VII, para. 3; see also Professor Asa Briggs, 'Social Background', in *The System of Industrial Relations in Great Britain*, Edited by Allan Flanders and H. A. Clegg, p.41 (1956).

VII

TECHNICAL EDUCATION

CONSIDERING that technical education for apprentices at large is a recent, post-war, development and that, unlike practical apprentice training, it is 'institutionalised', one might have expected it to be a rational system, functioning perhaps not yet faultlessly, but on the whole efficiently in adaptation to modern needs. In actual fact, our findings agree with what is by now the general verdict, that technical education of apprentices has so far not been a success.[1]

Most of the difficulties which beset the apprentices' technical education can be mainly ascribed to the rough-and-ready manner in which technical courses were joined to apprenticeship, a knocking together rather than a dovetailing of pieces. Many individuals and bodies, facilities and regulations, interests, agreements and customs are involved in the integration of technical education in apprenticeship; and the lack of co-ordination which is apparent at many points is bound to preclude satisfactory results. The chief points of non-articulation are:—

Apprenticeship is completed without a proof of proficiency, by mere lapse of time—technical courses are completed by examinations.

Day release for technical education of apprentices was agreed upon when statutory day release for all young workers was thought to be imminent through the Education Act, 1944

[1] The draft of our report was completed before the publication of *Technical Education and Social Change* by Stephen F. Cotgrove, in 1958. His book, while mainly concerned with the training of scientists and technologists, throws light on the technical education of apprentices of all grades.

—employers of apprentices, bearing the cost of day release, are liable to grudge it since it has not become a general statutory obligation.

The Ministry of Labour, through the strong arm of the Deferment Board, has pursued the drive for apprentices' attendance at day-release courses—facilities for technical education (college places and teachers) which are the responsibility of the L.E.As have been entirely insufficient for such a large influx of students.[1]

The prevailing arrangements for day release derive from desiderata for general further education, not from the requirements of technical education, viz:—

day release up to 18 makes available two years for apprentices' technical education—courses for C. & G. Intermediate and for O.N.C. examinations are planned for three years' part-time study;

day release is in terms of the apprentice's age (birthday)—the session of colleges begins in September;

release on one day per week may suit general further education—technical education benefits from longer spells of continuous study.

Technical colleges (together with day continuation schools) are meant to admit all apprentices—the selection of apprentices is at the discretion of the employers—the colleges' courses are governed by syllabuses which were laid down for examinees of a different calibre.

The principles of voluntarism and of equal opportunity[2] give the choice of course to the apprentice (or his employer) irrespective of the apprentice's educational attainment—the regulations for N.C. courses stipulate that only educationally qualified students are to be admitted to them.

The main weaknesses of the arrangements to make technical education an integral part of apprenticeship lie in the first and

---

[1] The Twelfth Report from the Select Committee on Estimates, 1952-53, on Technical Education, after quoting the M.o.E. 1947 Pamphlet No. 8, 'Further Education' on ' the very great dearth of accommodation' and 'most unsuitable premises', states that 'in spite of the money already expended on new construction, the position is still roughly the same as it was in 1947' (pp. ix and x).

[2] As expressed in the Education Act of 1944. See below, p. 133.

the last items of the foregoing list: in the fact that technical education, let alone the successful passing of an examination, is not a prerequisite for completing apprenticeship; and in the pressure of circumstances and aspirations which cause apprentices to attend courses which are too difficult for their capacity and also, in the opinion of many, on a higher level than is required for their future work.

During the period of this enquiry, important developments and changes have taken place in the field of technical education. There can be little doubt that considerable improvement is under way, since the alterations aim at reducing or abolishing many of the obstacles set up by the lack of co-ordination. But in some important respects, little or no progress has so far been made, and there seems to be a danger that new regulations will perpetuate old evils. The main recent developments in the field of technical education are mentioned in the following pages as occasion arises.

It is not easy to give an accurate picture of the conditions prevailing in technical education, not only because the organisation of technical education is in a state of rapid flux, but also because the statistical information is utterly deficient. The dearth of relevant statistical data and the manner in which they are presented cast a veil over the unsatisfactory state of affairs, but they arouse the investigator's suspicion.

The records of the College of Technology, Bristol, afford a certain amount of insight, and some information is contained in the B.A.C.'s Training Report which is published annually. The records of some colleges in other parts of the country are fuller than is required for the statistical returns (16 F.E.) to the Ministry of Education. In the last few years, material from such records (and data obtained by searching college registers) has been analysed and published in a number of articles and books.[1] These (mostly small) samples make it possible to appreciate the magnitude of the wastage in apprentices' technical

[1] To mention only some of the earliest: A. J. Jenkinson, 'S.1 Examinations in Mechanical Engineering' in *The Vocational Aspect of Secondary and Further Education,* Autumn, 1955 (Vol. VII, p.142/7); Professor Lady Williams, *op. cit.,* pp.162/7 (1957); C. B. Frisby, 'Apprentices' in *Technology: the Monthly Review of Training and Education for Industry,* published by *The Times,* Vol. 1, p.306 (November, 1957); Dr. Ethel C. Venables, ' Wasted Apprentices', ibid., p.392.

education. They show high failure rates in the various examinations, high proportions of students who do not even sit the appropriate examinations, and/or the frequency of students' 'repeats' of one or more years of a course.

Bristol has a twofold claim to be called a pioneer in technical education. First, 'The Trade School', opened in 1856 by the trustees of a disused Diocesan school, 'where youths of limited means could be provided with suitable training for an industrial career . . . [was] the first school in England that aimed at teaching the scientific principles upon which trades and manufactures are based'.[1] In 1885 it was taken over by the Society of Merchant Venturers, moved to new buildings and renamed Merchant Venturers' School.

Second, Bristol became, in the late 1870's, the birthplace of what are now called Sandwich Courses.[2] In the 1922 edition of his *Principles of Economics*, Alfred Marshall wrote :

'A good plan is that of spending the six winter months of several years after leaving school in learning science in College, and the six summer months as articled pupils in large workshops. The present writer introduced this plan about forty years ago at University College, Bristol (now the University of Bristol).'[3]

Following up this remark, we found that at the meeting of Council of 14th March, 1878,

'the Principal submitted a scheme respecting the teaching of Engineers at the College and read a report of a meeting . . . [between a sub-committee of Council] and representatives of Engineering firms in Bristol.'[4]

The Calendar, 1878–79, of the University College, Bristol, offered the following course.

[1] G. W. Charles, 'The Merchant Venturers' Technical College, Bristol' in *The Vocational Aspect*, Vol. III (1951), p.86/87.

[2] Scotland, however, was not far behind: 'The sandwich course was started in Glasgow Royal Technical College in 1880' (Mr. J. G. George in the House of Commons: *Hansard*, 21st June, 1956, col. 1683).

[3] P.209, footnote 3—Professor Marshall was the first Principal of University College, Bristol.

[4] Minute Book (starting 14th September, 1876), p.82; in the safe-keeping of the Registrar of the University of Bristol.

TECHNICAL EDUCATION

The instruction in this department is designed to afford a thorough scientific education for students intending to become Mechanical or Civil Engineers, Surveyors or Architects. The course for Engineering is such that students can pursue it during the six winter months of each year, and the Council of the College have arranged with the following Civil and Manufacturing Engineers to receive in their offices and workshops, during the summer months, students whose position relatively to the firms would be that of articled pupils. Engineering students can obtain a statement of the premium required, and any further information on application to the following firms. . . .'

Of eleven firms listed, ten were in Bristol, one in Bath. The sandwich course in engineering was a success, and in 1891 'the number of students wishing to take Engineering exceeded that which the space would accommodate. Decided to fix forty as maximum'.[1]

Meanwhile, the Merchant Venturers' School developed and assumed, in 1894, the style 'Technical College'. After the first World War, the Bristol Education Committee slowly increased its share in the responsibility for technical education. In 1936, the city decided to erect a new technical college; a site was bought, but no building plans had been made when war broke out in 1939. In 1949, the city bought the old college buildings from the Merchant Venturers Society and took over the control of the college.[2] The move of the college to its new premises was completed only in 1956, twenty years after the decision to build.

It was in these circumstances, that the B.A.C., with a growing demand for skilled personnel under the R.A.F. expansion programme in the later 1930s, proceeded to build its own works school. The first apprentice school at Filton (in Gloucestershire, just outside Bristol) was opened in 1938. By 1950, when the B.A.C.'s apprentices totalled 700, this works

---

[1] 'History of Engineering in University College, Bristol', p.6. Document No. 13, typed, in a collection of documents on the early days of the University; in the safe-keeping of the University Librarian.
[2] Source: G. W. Charles, l.c., p.88.

school provided C. & G. courses for all the firm's trade apprentices and O.N.C. courses for the majority of its Engineering apprentices. The rest attended courses at the Bristol College of Technology. The B.A.C.'s intake of apprentices continued to grow, and in 1953, the building of the present, larger Apprentice School began. By now, all O.N.C. students among the firm's apprentices attend at the works school.[1] H.N.C. students among B.A.C. apprentices, however, continue to enrol at the Bristol College; this is stipulated by the Ministry of Education (the B.A.C. school is 50% grant-aided) so that Advanced courses are concentrated at the College of Technology.

TECHNICAL EDUCATION FOR BRISTOL APPRENTICES AT THE TIME OF ENQUIRY

Technical education for Bristol apprentices is provided for in the first place by the Bristol College of Technology. The College's departments which cater for the three industries under review are the School of Printing, the Department of Engineering[2] and the Department of Building. The Bristol College is typical of English technical institutions in two respects: first, it provides instruction at divers levels—as wide apart as courses for trade apprentices and advanced professional courses—'the same formidable spread which one encounters in many technical colleges'.[3] Second, apprentices and/or their employers have, on the whole, been allowed to choose the level of course they are to attend.[4] This system contrasts with the organisation of technical education in other countries where students of different educational standards attend different technical colleges.

The ease of admission to part-time day courses of the Bristol College of Technology is not equal in all departments. The School of Printing and the Department of Building admit

---

[1] Source: Various B.A.C. reports.

[2] Although since 1956, there have been two engineering departments, of electrical and mechanical engineering respectively, the singular is retained in the following pages.

[3] Arthur Pennington, 'Technical Training in H.M. Forces' in *Vocational Aspect*, Spring, 1957, p.58.

[4] Recent changes in this respect are discussed on p. 130 below.

all apprentices in the respective trades. The Engineering Department, by contrast, puts an entrance test to apprentices whose certificates or school reports do not show them to have a minimum educational standard.

While the problems of technical education are greatest and most numerous for the engineering department, the printing and building departments have each some particular problems of their own, and some problems are common to all.

Printing
Although technical education is not a condition of apprenticeship in the printing trades, day release is the rule. At the instigation of the master printers of Bristol, part-time day classes had been opened at the Merchant Venturers' College in 1930.

Because of the small number of apprentices allowed by the apprentice ratios in the printing trades, technical colleges with printing departments are few and far between. The Bristol School of Printing has therefore a large catchment area, not only for the more advanced work.

Bristol printing firms release their apprentices on one half-day per week (a five-day week is worked) for the attendance of technical courses, as against the whole day per week recommended in the National Scheme ; in addition, apprentices have to attend evening classes in their own time, twice a week. The time given to technical education is $7\frac{1}{2}$ hours per week in the first two years and 7 hours thereafter; only 3 hours of this time are contributed by the 'half-day', so that the greater part falls into the evening.

For apprentices coming from a distance, the Bristol School of Printing runs courses of one whole day and evening per week, with 3 sessions, 9 a.m.—12 noon, 1.30—4.30, and 6—8 p.m., totalling eight hours per week. Some printing firms in rural areas, however, do not give their apprentices day release— attendance at classes is not, after all, compulsory. More than one such an employer, though, finds it useful to send an apprentice to Bristol for a short full-time course in Monotype casting.

The Bristol School of Printing has part-time day courses for four trades, viz. compositors, letterpress machinists, litho-graphic printers and book binders; a fifth course, in photo-graphic processes, has to be given in the evening (until 9 p.m. in the first year, until 8 p.m. in the second year of the course) because no teacher could be found for classes during working hours. (Day classes started in the session 1956/57). Litho-artist apprentices, finally, attend part-time day courses at the West of England College of Art.

We found consensus of opinion lacking regarding the subjects to be taught. While the School of Printing sets store by classes in English and Arithmetic, preferably at a time of the day when the students are not tired, employers, especially large firms, wish instruction during 'their time' to be purely in printing techniques. In deference to this wish, the courses for Bristol apprentices devote the half-day entirely to typography and composition (for compositor apprentices), or to letterpress machine work and printing-machine mechanics (for machinist apprentices), and so forth for other apprentices. English or general knowledge are the subjects of one of the evening classes, for compositors for the first two years, for machinist apprentices for one; lithographers have no such classes at all. By contrast, the apprentices coming to the School from farther afield for a whole day-cum-evening, take English and calculations or mechanics during the morning.

Another controversial matter is the introduction into the course of science subjects. Teachers complained that older supervisors in firms often discourage as useless theorizing the apprentices' interest in chemistry and other modern develop-ments related to printing.

The apprentices' progress in the first three years of their C. & G. courses—there are no other ones—is, so far as the available data permit to judge, steady in comparison with that of apprentice builders and engineers; a fairly high proportion of apprentice printers appear to reach the Inter-mediate C. & G. examination, some even the Final. However, the number attending courses falls sharply from the third to the fourth years, the main cause being that about half of the printing apprentices chose not to claim deferment of their call-up. Success in the sessional examinations of the School and for the C. & G. certificates is rewarded by prizes by the Master Printers' Association but does not lead to higher wages; and the completion of apprenticeship is in no way dependent on it.

The syllabus of the course for machinist apprentices is another confirmation of the view that the work of the machine-minder, whether in letterpress, lithography or photogravure work, has become almost indistinguishable from engineers' work. Printing is being done by ever more complicated machinery and the machine-minders have, therefore, to learn mechanics and science.

Building

The standards set for the technical education of trowel-trade apprentices are too severe to be realistic. The day-cum-evening courses which are obligatory for the apprentice until the age of 18 should enable him to pass at this age at least the C. & G. Intermediate examination which is to be taken after the second-year part-time course; at best, i.e. if he starts at 15 and makes steady progress, he should be half-way through the course for the Final examination which is taken after the fourth-year course. But this is not what usually happens. To begin with, the building employers' obligation to release apprentices during working hours has so far not applied to the probation period. It has been a not uncommon practice, therefore, to keep a boy of 15 on probation for the allowed maximum of six months, and if this period ends after Easter, say, the apprentice would not begin his technical education before the college's new session starts in the autumn. He thus experiences the same educational gap as those who enter apprenticeship at 16.

While all building apprentices are admitted to the College, they have to sit for a grading test and are allocated to different streams according to ability. A high proportion of apprentices —not only in the trowel trades—make slow progress: instead of moving to the next higher class each session, they have to repeat the year, many more than once. Some students are promoted to the next higher 'year-group' but transferred to a lower stream. Few succeed in passing the Intermediate, and a very small proportion of trowel-trade apprentices pass the Final C. & G. examination.

In the absence, not only for Bristol, of accurate statistical data, the City and Guilds of London Institute has made a 'very rough' but helpful quantitative assessment of the performance of building craft apprentices in technical college courses.[1] The assessment suggests that, in 1955, of the apprentice bricklayers in the respective age group, just over one-quarter passed the Intermediate examination and not quite one-tenth the Final examination; of the apprentice plasterers, only one-tenth passed the former and one-thirtieth the latter examination. These proportions compare rather unfavourably with those in carpentry and in plumbing, where not much less than one-half of the apprentices passed the Intermediate, and between one-fifth and one-fourth the Final examination.

Of late, however, we are told, day release during the probation period is more generally given, and this will become obligatory as the result of a revision of the National Scheme which is under way. The C. & G. syllabuses for building subjects are also being revised; the Intermediate examination (after the second-year course) is to be discontinued and a three-year course will lead to a new basic craft certificate which, it is hoped, will be obtained by 60% of the apprentices.

The stipulation that building-trade apprentices are to continue classes on two evenings a week after the age of 18 has likewise proved to be over-exacting. Enrolment is far below 100%, and among those who enrol, absenteeism is about 30%. One of the large Bristol building firms relieves its apprentices from the obligation to continue technical education in the evenings by giving them day release until the end of their apprenticeship. There is some evidence, however, that these apprentices exploit their employer's generosity; and it is perhaps some of them who, according to an eager apprentice, do not want to learn anything themselves and spoil the classes for those who want to.

In plastering, the director of the leading Bristol plastering firm has for years been concerned with the wastefulness of technical education: each C. & G. certificate obtained was costing the plastering industry £1,000 because all apprentices

[1] B.A.T.C., *Final Report*, Appendix 3.

have to be given day release, but only a tiny minority reach, and are successful in, the examinations. A frequent complaint by plasterer apprentices, on the other hand, is that of over-training; they consider neither free-hand drawing nor intricate ornamental plastering as of any use or interest to them, nor mathematics as within their capacity.

In 1956, day release of plasterers was experimentally converted into 'block release' (such a scheme, a sort of sandwich course for craft apprentices, had been in existence for a couple of years for heating and ventilating engineers who belong, in Bristol, to the College's Building Department). This alternative to release on one day per week had been provided for in the Education Act of 1944, Section 44 (3b), viz. one continuous period of eight weeks, or two continuous periods of four weeks each, in every year.

The first-year block release course of eight weeks was attended in 1956 by 14 apprentice plasterers from the Bristol and Bath areas and was considered a success as a form of training. Although the small number of apprentices attending the courses is disappointing, the block-release system has been adopted for all four years. The courses are now organised in two four-week periods, as it was felt that eight weeks' continuous technical instruction was too long a spell for plasterers.

As already pointed out, the requirements as to day release under the National Apprenticeship Scheme for the Building Industry have been one of the main reasons for the opposition to the Scheme by small building firms, who train a high proportion of all building apprentices without the sanction of the industry's National Scheme.

Engineering

In Engineering, to recapitulate, apprentices' day release for attendance at technical courses is neither mandatory as in Building, nor 'strongly recommended' as in Printing. The picture is therefore one of very great disparity. Employers' policy ranges from not granting day release to making atten-dance at day classes compulsory for their apprentices. The inclusion or non-inclusion of a clause on technical classes in the indenture form used by an employer is no indication of the actual policy followed by him: some employers using the B.E.M.A. form, which provides for day release, do not send their apprentices to technical day classes; whereas some firms using the Engineering Employers' Association form, which does not mention further education, are giving their apprentices day release.

Employers' attitude to day release has been governed by two considerations:—the value which they put on technical education, and the knowledge that day release helps to secure the deferment of the apprentice's call-up for National Service.

Most employers release apprentices under 18 for the attendance of technical courses. Since, on the whole, the large firms do so, it may be safely assumed that the great majority of apprentices attend a part-time day course before they attain the age of 18. But this does not mean that all of them attend for the full two years from 16 to 18: firms, not all of them small, were found to reduce the period of day release to one year or less, either by letting it start only after an apprentice has passed the technical college's first sessional examination by study in evening classes, or else by withdrawing day release from apprentices who fail in the first sessional examination. Some employers, mainly in the case of not-so-bright apprentices, refuse to give them day release and get away with it, even though, as one of them put it, they may 'have a bit of trouble in obtaining deferment for them'. In the opinion of such employers, technical education for future shopfloor craftsmen is not necessary, or even quite unnecessary and 'beyond their station in life'.

At the other end of the scale, the B.A.C. makes practically all its apprentices attend technical courses during working hours up to the completion of their apprenticeship. Most firms' attitude to technical education is somewhere between the two extremes. At the Westinghouse Company, the proportion attending technical courses during working hours was, in 1956, 80% of all apprentices. Some not so large firms, too, continue to give day release to apprentices after they reach the age of 18, even to those who make slow progress.

While firms differ widely in their attitude to day release of apprentices at large, there is remarkable uniformity regarding day release for the attendance of higher courses. A firm may deny day release for C. & G. courses but readily give it for attendance at N.C. courses. This matter is discussed from a different angle in the latter part of this chapter. It should, however, be mentioned here that we have been told by the staff of more than one technical college that a firm is too often unaware of the outstanding theoretical ability of one of its apprentices or ex-apprentices and fails to give him greater opportunities of training and, later, to promote him to a position where his capability can be fully used.

Another divergence of opinion between college and the employers of apprentices is about the growing practice of technical colleges to include practical instruction in the courses. The most obvious purpose of this is to make up for the small range or out-dated models of machines with which apprentices in some smaller firms get acquainted. Some large modern firms protest against this policy of the technical college, because their apprentices can get to know diverse modern machines in the works, and want the apprentices' time at the college to be spent entirely on technical and theoretical subjects (this is also recommended in the specimen Syllabuses). The colleges' rejoinder is that in modern industrial conditions productive work and apprentice training cannot efficiently be done together.

Apprentices' attitude to technical education ranges from keenness to boredom and even dread. An unwilling trade apprentice may manage to keep away from classes; professing that the instruction is of no use to him, he may get his employer's agreement to foregoing further education; by irregular attendance, by lack of interest and application he can cause the Technical College to refuse him re-admission. The College, while it cannot force apprentices to attend, can exclude them from its courses. Obviously much depends on the employer's interest in his apprentices' technical education.

The complaint we heard most frequently from apprentices on their technical instruction is that it does not tie up with their practical work; further, that courses are too theoretical, proceed too fast, pack too much in. On the other hand, a number of our apprentice interviewees, especially N.C. students, found the technical course close to their practical work and giving them a broader view: 'The classes help you to think in an engineering way', said a maintenance fitter apprentice; and 'I always know what they [on the shopfloor] are getting at' was the appreciation of his technical course by a general-engineering apprentice.

A different aspect of apprentices' attitude to technical education will be discussed presently, viz. the remarkable 'popularity' of N.C. courses.

Passing from the consumers to the purveyors of technical education, we have to deal mainly with two institutions, the *College of Technology, Bristol*, and the *Apprentice School of the B.A.C.* It should be called to mind that, for a variety of reasons, the B.A.C. is foremost among the small number of local firms that take the cream of the recruits for apprenticeships in engineering. The applicants for places in the college's engineering department exclude therefore the apprentices recruited, as the most promising ones, by the B.A.C. and whose technical education, except for Advanced courses, is catered for by the company's works school.

It is to the *Engineering Department of the College of Technology* that apprentice engineers who are indentured with other firms than the B.A.C. (including apprentice maintenance engineers in non-engineering firms) look for the provision of technical courses. Bristol, which had planned to erect a new technical college in 1936 found its accommodation sorely inadequate to cope with the sudden post-war demand for places which resulted from the Government's drive for apprentices' day-release courses. Moreover, the College of Technology being a Regional College (with the prospect of graduation to the status of a College of Advanced Technology)[1], its engineering department is particularly interested in developing Senior and Advanced professional and technological courses, whereas, in the words of the College prospectus, technical and craft courses are ' also available.'

Out of concern for minimum standards, and hard-pressed for accommodation, the department has for many years put to an entrance test apprentices whose educational qualification seemed doubtful; neither their numbers nor the proportions

[1] Sir David Eccles in House of Commons, 21st June, 1956. *Hansard*, col. 1664.

rejected were obtainable. In September, 1955, when for the first time all new part-time day students were subjected to a grading test, almost half of them were not admitted but were advised to attend the Day Continuation School; from the statistical data available about the D.C.S. it is, however, clear that this advice was disregarded by many of the rejects and/or their employers: a few such apprentices, employed outside Bristol, are known to receive special coaching in mathematics in the evening by arrangement of their firm; others may go to evening classes or take a correspondence course; an unknown number must be assumed to remain without Further Education.

A stage intermediate between rejection and admittance to the department's ordinary courses is the entering of apprentices into a one-year Preliminary Engineering Course; these courses consisting of classes in mathematics and science, are held on Saturdays, plus one evening a week for drawing.[1]

For the apprentices who are admitted to the engineering department, the essential division of courses is between Craft courses in preparation for City and Guilds examinations in various trades, and Senior courses leading to Ordinary National Certificates in Mechanical or Electrical Engineering.

Until 1955, apprentices who were admitted enrolled for courses more or less according to their own or their employers' wishes, irrespective of their educational standards. This freedom of choice was in line with the regulation in the Education Act of 1944 for further education in general;[2] and it was a not

[1] In 1957 the Preliminary Course was removed from the College and, renamed 'Pre-Senior Technical Course', is now one of the Day Continuation Classes, the new name of the D.C.S., which has also been rehoused, enlarged and re-organised. The one-year ' Pre-Senior' course prepares for admission to either C. & G. or O.N.C. courses at the College of Technology; a new 'Preliminary Technical Course' at the D.C. Classes is taken by 15-year old boys who may be promoted to the pre-senior course after one term; thirdly, a General Studies Course caters for non-technical day-release students, including Post Office employees and Juniors in Civil Service departments.

Another recent development which increases the facilities for technical education in the Bristol area, and simultaneously helps the College of Technology to shed its junior courses, is the inauguration, by the Gloucestershire Education Committee, of an Engineering Department in the Bristol Fringe Area, namely in the Kingswood College of Boot and Shoe Manufacture. Since the session 1956/7, Greater Bristol has thus the beginnings of a Local Technical College in addition to the Regional College of Technology.

[2] See p. 133 below.

unimportant factor in determining the conditions of apprentices' technical education which prevailed during the period of this enquiry. A considerable modification in the admission of students to courses of different levels began in the session 1955/56 and is described on p. 131 below.

The craft courses available in Bristol are in the usual subjects of the City and Guilds syllabuses, Machine Shop Engineering, Motor Vehicle Work, Electrical Installation, and so forth. (Machine Shop Engineering is the course for such basic trades as fitter and turner; it was started in Bristol only in 1952). The Intermediate City and Guilds examination is taken after the third-year course (except in Electrical Installation where the examination after the third-year course is the only examination).

National Certificate courses are at two levels: a three-year course for Ordinary Certificates and an additional two-year course for Higher Certificates.

The several levels of the courses at the technical college are at first sight parallel with the grading of apprenticeships by some firms. Craft apprenticeship appears to correspond to the City and Guild courses, Engineering apprenticeship to the Ordinary National Certificate courses, Undergraduate apprenticeship to courses at University level, with Higher National Certificate courses somewhere between the last two. In actual fact, the correspondence is weak: a considerable number of craft apprentices attend courses which prepare for N.C. examinations, without having the mental capacity or the educational attainment, particularly in mathematics, to profit from these courses. Before dealing with this important topic, we must attempt to draw some information from the available statistical data, meagre as they are.

As repeatedly stated, the statistical information on technical education is very poor. The total number of day-release students in the college's engineering department was, in the years under review, of the order of 1,500 ; but, on the one hand, this total includes non-apprentices, e.g. employees of the Gas Board and of the Post Office who are released for C. & G. courses in gas-fitting and telecommunication respectively, further a number of pre-apprentices; on the other hand, it excludes by definition those genuine apprentices for whom no day courses were then available, e.g. sheet-metal workers. Information is not available on the annual intake of each course; on the number of students who repeat, once or several times, one or more years of a course; nor, without laborious extractions, on the number or proportions of students in courses of different levels: preliminary —C. & G.—N.C. courses.[1] The age distribution of the day-release students is not broken down for individual courses.

Both the age distribution and the proportions of students attending at courses of different levels are influenced by the fact that the Bristol College of Technology is a Regional College: the numbers in its higher courses and older age groups are increased by students coming for more advanced study from outlying places (and also from the B.A.C.), whereas more junior courses can be attended in smaller towns (and also in the B.A.C.'s Apprentice School); there are also the local grammar-school boys who enter apprenticeship at 17 or 18, with higher educational qualifications: they start at the college in S.2, i.e. the second year of the O.N.C. course.

In spite of all these qualifications and uncertainties, the college lists of students and the L.E.A.'s annual statistical returns to the Ministry of Education yield a measure of numerical information on some relevant aspects over which published official statistics draw a veil.[2]

The following table shows the number of students in each year of various three-year courses in 1954/5.

---

[1] The definition in the '16 F.E.' returns ('Return for a Major Establishment for Further Education') of courses as Junior, Senior or Advanced is ambiguous, and the college's interpretation of 'Senior' is inconsistent with the prevailing description of technical-education courses. The equivocal classification of courses appears to be the accepted practice of technical colleges; as regards this classification, therefore, the table which summarizes the 16 F.E. Returns for England and Wales in the Ministry of Education's annual Reports (Table 52 in *Education in 1956* Cmd. 223) is useless and even misleading.

It is suggestive that the instructions for the completion of the 16 F.E. forms include an assurance that 'these classifications are for statistical purposes and are not related to the definitions in . . . the Report of the Burnham Committee on Scales of Salaries'—see below, p. 134,

[2] An amended version of the Returns came into use for the Session 1956/7 (there are now two forms, 16 F.E. and 16ª F.E.). However, while there is some improvement, none of the shortcomings in the statistics which are pointed out in the text and the footnote above have been remedied.

Table I: Day-release students, 1954/5

Department of Engineering, Bristol College of Technology

(a) C. & G. Courses[1]

Year of Course	Machine Shop Engineering		Motor Vehicle Mechanics		Electrical Installation		All three Courses
	No.	Index	No.	Index	No.	Index	No.
1st	66	= 100	56	= 100	91	= 100	213
2nd	43	65	50	89	33	36	126
3rd	16	24	31	55	28	31	75
4th	—		17	30			17
5th	—		—				
Total	125		154		152		431

(b) 'Senior'[2] O.N.C. Courses

	Mechanical Engineering		Electrical Engineering		Both Courses
	No.	Index	No.	Index	No.
S.1	187	= 100	88	= 100	275
S.2	153	82	67	76	220
S.3	126	67	27	31	153
Total	466		182		648

One outstanding feature is the small number of C. & G. students compared with students in N.C. courses. The college's engineering department, we were told in 1956, does 'not go in much for C. & G. examinations'; in the session 1956/7, the proportion of students taking craft courses to those taking N.C. courses was given as approximately one to two, but said to be increasing.

Another salient feature, common, if in varying degrees, to all courses, is the preponderance of the number of students in

[1] The three courses shown are the main C. & G. courses for apprentices; three others, in Radio Service Work, Foundry Work and Patternmaking, with a combined total of 69 students, had not yet developed a third-year course.

[2] i.e. excluding 'Advanced' courses which lead to the H.N.C.

the first-year courses. This might have several causes: a steady annual increase of the intake of first-year students; the discontinuation of attendance at day-time technical courses after one year's attendance; and failure in the sessional examination so that the first-year course has to be repeated. The available information makes it only imperfectly possible to gauge the comparative importance of these causes.

It is more than probable, however, that the main cause is the repetition of a year's course. We were given to understand that it is exceptional rather than the rule for a C. & G. course student to proceed without having to repeat at least one year. This is confirmed by the considerable number of apprentices of 18 and 19 years of age who were found to attend the first and second-year courses in Machine Shop Engineering and in Motor Vehicle Work.

In the Motor Vehicle Mechanics course the number of students is much better maintained from one year to the next than in the other craft courses. This may be at least partly due to a particular incentive. A National Craftsman's Certificate for Motor Vehicle Service Mechanics is awarded by the Ministry of Education in conjunction with the National Joint Council for the trade, and a pass in the City and Guilds examination is recognised in respect of the apprentice's theoretical knowledge. (There is also a National Craftsman's Certificate for Gauge and Tool Makers, but Bristol does not participate in this scheme).

In the N.C. courses at the college, the reduction of numbers attending over the years of a course is apparently smaller than in the C. and G. courses. But S.2 has a fresh influx of holders of the G.C.E. (A level)[1]; moreover, during the period of our investigation the Bristol Aeroplane Company was gradually withdrawing its apprentices from the O.N.C. courses of the college: in 1954/5, no B.A.C. students attended S.1; four attended S.2, and twenty-three S.3 (all in Mechanical Engineering). Table 1(b) is therefore of little use in this respect. However, investigations based on fuller records of N.C. students at other colleges leave no doubt that repetition, at least once and at least of one year of a course, has been a

[1] See p. 130 below.

general disease of technical education. Official statistical data are not available, but a question about the repetition of any year of the O.N.C. course is included in the questionnaire of a sample survey now being made by the Advisory Council for Education (England) under the chairmanship of Sir Geoffrey Crowther.

The Annual Training Reports of the *B.A.C.* show 'End of Session Examination Results' which provide valuable, if not full, information on failure rates. The data are not only detailed as to differentiation of courses and inclusion of sessional, in addition to certificate, examinations, but are particularly instructive because of their wide coverage. The usual presentation of examination results juxtaposes the number who enter (or sit for) an examination and the number who pass, but leaves in the dark the number of students who ought to have entered the examination, but did not in fact do so; the value of such examination statistics is rather limited. The B.A.C. figures, by contrast, are fairly comprehensive. In the accompanying Table 2, we have computed the failure rates in the main C. & G. course, Machine Shop Engineering, and in the N.C. course in Mechanical Engineering as percentages of the totals sitting for each examination. Since the great majority (well over 90%, it would seem) of all B.A.C. apprentices sit for the appropriate sessional or certificate examination each year, the failure rates in the table indicate with fair accuracy the frequency of failure among the apprentices in the respective stages of each course. The fact that, at the B.A.C., an indifferent student cannot easily avoid the annual examinations must be remembered in an interpretation of the B.A.C. failure rates.

All the same, the failure rates are high. In 14 out of 49 examinations shown in the tables more than half of the examinees failed, and only in 5 of the 49 examinations was the failure rate less than a quarter. Surely, something must have been wrong, if this could happen to a firm which has the pick of apprentices, applies elaborate selection methods and devotes particular effort and care to the apprentices' technical education in its own works school? (The examination results of the diminishing number of B.A.C. apprentices who attend O.N.C. courses at the Bristol College of Technology affect, but do not essentially change the picture).

TABLE 2: END OF SESSION EXAMINATION RESULTS, B.A.C.

(a) C. & G. course in Machine Shop Engineering (at the B.A.C. Apprentice School)

Failure Rates
(Failures as % of Total Sitting for Examination)

Year	Intermediate Course			Final Course	
	1st yr.	2nd yr.	3rd yr.	4th yr.	5th yr.
1951/2	29	36	67	71	—
52/3	67	49	33*	69	45*
53/4	42	14	23*	27	75*
54/5	51	36	37*	52	55*
55/6	39	62	30*	48	43*

(b) N.C. Courses† in Mechanical Engineering‡

Failure Rates
(Failures as % of Total Sitting for Examination)

Year	'Senior' O.N.C. Course			'Advanced' H.N.C. Course	
	1st year S.1	2nd yr. S.2	3rd yr. S.3	1st yr. A.1	2nd yr. A.2
1951/2	54	41	35	47	24
52/3	26	49	34	40	16
53/4	58	38	42	52	59
54/5	22	52	42	39	42
55/6	35	30	49	28	31

* Excluding N.C. students taking these C. & G. examinations.

† O.N.C. courses (i) at B.A.C. Apprentice School, (ii) at Bristol College of Technology; H.N.C. course only at the College: see p. 114. The failure rates are computed here for the total B.A.C. apprentices taking these courses; the firm's Annual Training Report gives separate figures for (i) and for (ii).

‡ Incl. Production Engineering.

The table shows very great variations in failure rates from year to year. The way in which the examination results are tabulated does not make possible a full explanation of these variations; but some can be accounted for. The high failure rate in 1953/4 in S.1, the first year of the O.N.C. course, was explained by the firm thus :

'A more liberal interpretation of the Institution of Mechanical Engineers' regulations has excused more new students from the first year of this course and they entered directly into the second year. The first-year classes have thus been deprived of what were previously their best students, so lowering the percentage passing the first-year examination.'[1]

The sequel is interesting. A year later, the company wrote:

'The lower percentage of passes in the second and third[2] years of the Ordinary National Certificate course is attributed to the practice of allowing all students qualified under the Institution of Mechanical Engineers' regulations to omit taking the first year of the course and entering direct upon the second year. In practice it has been found that a number of these students do not have a sufficient grounding to carry them successfully to the Ordinary National Certificate. This session, therefore, a domestic grading examination was used in the selection for direct entry into the second year of the course and a larger proportion of the new students than in the past entered the first year.'[3]

In this way it was hoped to ensure better results from the National Certificate courses. In its latest Report the Company finds itself not dissatisfied with the 1956 results; the S.3 result still reflects the now discarded policy of easy direct admission to the second year of the course; the higher failure rate in S.1 is not commented upon.

Besides, the B.A.C. has been striving to improve the examination results by more radical reforms. An important measure was the re-arrangement, in 1956, of the timing of technical education. Day-release courses had not been conducive to success in examinations; therefore, instead of one day

---

[1] B.A.C., Annual Training Report 1954, p.8.

[2] At the Company school, the failure rate in S.3 was 41% in 1954/5 as against 22% in 1953/4; this rise is obscured in table 2(b) through our drawing together the results of B.A.C. apprentices studying at the Company School and at the College of Technology.

[3] Annual Training Report, 1955, p.6.—Note that the educational standard for B.A.C. apprentices who take O.N.C. courses is the G.C.E. with six passes at ordinary level; the new domestic examination for exemption from S.1 is in addition to that qualification.

per week, trade apprentices now go to school for one whole week in every four (which gives not only more continuity, but also slightly more time for technical education), and Engineering apprentices attend sandwich courses of six months every year.

Furthermore, the fight against high failure rates has been carried into the lines of the examining bodies: the B.A.C. has joined those who demand a revision of the contents of the O.N.C. courses[1]—the chief controversy is about the required standard in mathematics.[2]

Meanwhile, the College of Technology too has become more discriminating in the drafting of apprentices into technical courses. Since 1955, the College's engineering department has made a large proportion of applicants sit for a grading test which consists of papers in mathematics and in English-cum-general knowledge. Allocation to courses is mainly based on the results of the examination in mathematics.

In thus trying to secure that only students with appropriate educational standards (no specific standards are laid down) are admitted to N.C. courses, the Bristol College conforms to a procedure which is now widely advocated.[3] The grading test should contribute towards reducing failure rates; but the experience of the B.A.C. makes it improbable that sufficient improvement will result from this measure alone. Moreover, as will be discussed presently, forces are at work which threaten a continued admission of students to courses above their educational capacities.

THE ASCENDANCY OF NATIONAL CERTIFICATE COURSES[4]

National Certificate courses were devised for the training of

[1] *Technology*, March, 1958, p.3 reports that the principal of the B.A.C. apprentice school 'spoke up . . . for a radical revision of the Ordinary National Certificate'.

[2] See, e.g., J. A. C. Williams, 'Attainment in N.C. Mathematics' in *Vocational Aspect*, Spring, 1957, p.13ff.

[3] The regulations for approval of National Certificate courses had from the beginning provided for such selective admission; see p. 39 above.

[4] See note on p.109 above. Our interpretation of the situation on the following pages is supported by Dr. Cotgrove's detailed and fully documented discussion of the policy in technical education of the professional institutions and of that of the Government (*op. cit.*, chapters 11-13).

'technicians and professional men', as distinct from craftsmen whose technical education has long been served by C. & G. courses. Since the last war, however, a very large number of craft apprentices have enrolled for N.C. courses. No official statistics showing the distribution of day-release students to C. & G. and to N.C. courses are available, but there can be no doubt about the 'dominating influence' of the National Certificate and 'its conquest of technical colleges'.[1] At some local colleges, N.C. courses have been the only ones available for day-release students, although nearly all of these were drawn from secondary modern schools.[2] The high failure rates in O.N.C. courses must be largely attributed to such a maladjustment of secondary and further education.

Yet the N.C. has been 'very popular'; in fact, there has been a strong preference for N.C. rather than for C. & G. courses among apprentices, their employers, colleges' engineering departments and L.E.As throughout the country. The question is, why?

The answer is comparatively easy as regards *apprentices*. Since the passing of an examination is not required for the successful completion of apprenticeship, a C. & G. examination is unnecessary to indifferent apprentices, and to the ambitious ones it is of little value, as it does not open the door to advancement. But by way of the National Certificates, the apprentice can reach semi-professional or even professional status. Having to attend day-release courses anyhow, many are attracted by the prestige of the N.C. and 'have a go at it'. However, by no means all apprentices who enlist for a N.C. course, although craft courses are available, do so on their own volition: many do so at the request of their employers.

The reasons why *firms* consider N.C. courses desirable for their craft apprentices are complex. Some of these apprentices are craft apprentices only in name; the grading of apprentices by employers has not yet become general practice. In firms where grading is not introduced, boys of promise are expected to rise to managerial status, whether as designer, production

---

[1] F. E. Foden, The National Certificate, in *Vocational Aspect*, May, 1951, p.38.
[2] See, e.g., S. Summersbee, 'Admission of Students to N.C. Courses', in *Vocational Aspect*, Spring, 1957, p.19.ff.

engineer or works manager; they may have had a grammar-school or technical-school education and may reasonably be expected to embark on a National Certificate course. After all, the N.C. schemes were 'designed to enable the best of young workers in industry to qualify themselves for promotion to the higher industrial ranks.'[1]

But some firms require *all* their apprentices to attend N.C. courses. This occurs where an employer considers that the City and Guild courses are not well run, or else that they duplicate the practical instruction which, he claims, his apprentices receive in the works. Other employers want in this way to test their apprentices' application and mental capacity, and they make those who do not stay the course step down to attend a craft course. Various training officers (not in the survey area) expressed the opinion, that everybody should be given the chance to go to the top, and that a man will be more content in a modest job after he has realised that he cannot make a higher grade. The distressing and demoralising effects of failure are not taken account of in this argument.

Technical colleges and the *L.E.As* which are responsible for them have one common reason for favouring N.C. courses for apprentices, viz. consideration of space, which is urgent in view of the pressure for places in the colleges: the more theoretical N.C. course requires less space per student than a C. & G. course which includes workshop practice.

In addition, there lingers among L.E.As the idea that under the motto 'equal opportunity for all' each boy should have the right to enrol in a course of study which may take him to a high position; this idea ignores the changes brought about by the Education Act of 1944 which aims at achieving equality of educational opportunity during secondary-school life. It is due to this idea that a clause on further education in general (Section 44 (7) of the 1944 Act) has been indiscriminately applied to the particular case of technical education :

'In determining . . . college attendance . . ., the L.E.A. shall have regard, as far as practicable, to any preference which [the young person] may express . . . and to representations . . . by his employer.'

[1] *Education in 1948*, Report of the Ministry of Education, p. 42.

As a consequence, apprentices have been able to opt for technical courses above the level of their educational qualification.

As regards the technical colleges, a variety of reasons and motives for favouring N.C. courses come into play: most teachers derive greater satisfaction from giving higher courses; the prestige of a college is enhanced by having many students enrolled for senior, advanced or 'post-advanced' courses; and the teachers' rank and salary hinge upon the level of their courses.[1]

The attitudes of the *examining bodies* for the two types of certificate have to be discussed separately.

The courses of the *City and Guilds of London Institute* have been driven to the wall. Their syllabuses were developed for examinations to be taken by the elite of the craftsmen. And this remained their standard, in spite of the twofold transformation which the technical education of apprentices has undergone during the last three decades. On the one hand, apprentices of theoretical aptitude and higher education are now studying for the National Certificate examinations; on the other hand, a large new category of examinee, of more practical bent, has come into being through the promotion of technical education for all apprentices. It is only slowly that the C. & G. syllabuses are beginning to be adjusted to the capacities and needs of the rank and file of trade apprentices.

However, the Department of Technology of the City and Guilds Institute renders an important service by regarding it as one of its main functions 'to receive and interpret the requirements of industry . . . and to reconcile these with educational principles and practices . . .'[2]. Such interpretation and reconciliation with principles are indeed necessary, for proposals for the development of new schemes or the alteration of existing ones so as to suit particular industries or localities may, from a wider view, have serious implications. For example, at

[1] The Burnham (Technical) Committee (1951 and 1954 Reports on Scales of Salaries for Teachers in Establishments for Further Education, Appendix VI) wishes the Local Education Authorities 'to determine the grading of posts so that the proportion of posts in the higher grades is in a right relationship to the proportions of work in the higher standards'.—See also p. 136f. below.

[2] C. & G. of London Institute, 76th Annual Report, 1954/1955, p.22.

a national conference of training officers it was suggested that the C. & G. syllabus for maintenance fitters should be focused on the needs of a given industry or section of industry rather than on the trade of a fitter. This might, it is true, benefit the employer and other firms in the same section of industry; but the ensuing narrow technical specialisation of the craftsman, in addition to the one-sidedness of his practical training, would reduce his choice of job and would impede the mobility of labour; and the narrowed syllabuses would frustrate the keener students among the apprentices.

The Professional Institutions

Apprentices who study for a National Certificate are taking part in a 'race of technical education'. From interviews with persons in different positions and from the pertinent literature one cannot help suspecting that the standard of the examinations for the N.Cs is being pushed up beyond what is required. The chief reason for this seems to be that the H.N.C. is used as a means of restricting entrance into the ranks of professionally qualified engineers. It is given the function which the masterpiece or 'proof-piece' had in the 16th and 17th centuries when it was 'used as a barrier against the flood of journeymen whom the masters desired to keep in the position of wage-earners.'[1] Although in the present industrial structure there are few masters, and most professional engineers are salaried employees, the professional institutions, the main controllers of N.C. examinations, endeavour to protect their members' interest against a flood of part-time students by making the entry into their ranks difficult by means of stiff examinations. 'This ever-rising spiral is now acquiring an even steeper gradient, so that it is becoming increasingly difficult for students to reach professional status through this part-time route.'[2]

These higher reaches of technical part-time education are attained by few apprentices. But the thesis propounded here is that indirectly the exacting standard set at the top raises also the standards at lower levels, so as to make the level of the

[1] George Unwin, *The Gilds and Companies of London*, p.266 (1908).
[2] P. F. R. Venables, *Technical Education*, p.158 (1955).

O.N.C. examination higher than warranted by the requirements of industry.

The thesis is supported by the professional institutions' protracted indifference to the high 'mortality rates' in N.C. examinations. In this respect, they have not exercised the control of N.C. courses which has been vested in them, jointly with the Ministry of Education, ever since the introduction of the first N.C. course, in Mechanical Engineering, in 1921, viz. to satisfy themselves as to the steps taken to secure that students are not admitted to the courses unless they are qualified to profit by them.

Nor did the Ministry of Education show concern about the high failure rates until it announced on 31st January, 1958 the decision to carry out a special enquiry into the wastage of students in some of the main part-time courses in technical colleges.[1]

GOVERNMENT POLICY

The Government not only maintains, but adds to, the existing profusion of technical courses and examinations by introducing new qualifications, such as the Dip. Tech.

Maybe the policy of maintaining and even increasing the multiformity of the technical-education system is partly explained by the desire not to interfere with the fight for position which is going on between engineers on various rungs of the ladder of technical qualification. In descending order, the grades are: Mathematics (or Science) Degree—Engineering Degree—Dip. Tech.—H.N.C.—O.N.C.—Craftsman (with or without C. & G. Certificate)—semi-skilled operative.

At the top and at the bottom of the ladder, competition between adjacent grades is intense; just as craftsmen are challenged by operatives,[2] engineering graduates are challenged by H.N.C. holders; and they fight on a second front against mathematicians as competitors for senior design posts.

The lower middle, the technicians', range seems at present to be the calmest zone; there is no competition by craftsmen as

---

[1] *Technology*, March, 1958, p.6.
[2] See p. 161ff below.

a group to fill technicians' posts (although individual craft apprentices strive for such positions and attempt to gain the O.N.C. for this purpose), and holders of the H.N.C. aspire to technologists' work and rank. It remains to be seen how the situation will be affected by the campaign for a great increase in the number of highly qualified engineers.

The Government takes, however, responsibility for the organisation of technical colleges; there are now four tiers, Local Colleges at the bottom, Colleges of Advanced Technology at the top, but there is no clear division between the levels of work to be done by each type of college. It is this lack of delimitation to which we referred at the beginning of this chapter[1] as jeopardizing the sound development of apprentices' technical education. The Government's countenance of colleges' endeavour to 'advance their status'[2] threatens with continued neglect the great many craft apprentices for whom C. & G. courses are the most suitable ones. The reason for the indifference to craft courses is that a college's advance in status (and a special rate of 75% grant) depends on the volume and proportion of its advanced work; Advanced, i.e. H.N.C., courses however grow out of O.N.C. courses, not out of C. & G. courses.

Would it not be in the public interest for there to be colleges whose full purpose would be the technical (and general) education, so essential in modern conditions, of the basic skilled manpower?

---

[1] P. 111; see also pp. 131 and 134.
[2] Ministry of Education, Circular 305, 21st June, 1956.

VIII

COMPLETION OF APPRENTICESHIP

THE AGE OF COMPLETION

THE normal length of apprenticeship is now five years, after it had for many centuries been seven years.[1] When the Ministry of Labour made its sample enquiry into apprenticeship in the mid-nineteen twenties, the seven-year term was on its way out. In 1925-26, 'the period most frequently served [was] five years, nearly twice as many boys serving for this period as for seven years . . .'[2] The shortening by two years of the former seven-year term takes place at the beginning: connected with the raising of the school-leaving age, apprenticeship starts later than formerly—it is not completed at an earlier age. The age of completion is the terminus *ad quem* for fixing the age of entry into apprenticeship.

Twenty-one years is the traditional age for completing craft apprenticeship. As the minimum age, it was stipulated by the Statute of Artificers,[3] was laid down by autonomous trade union rules, and is at present a clause in most National Apprenticeship Schemes. But 21 years has also long been the maximum age for the completion of apprenticeship. The fixing of 16 years as the upper age for beginning apprenticeship and the stipulated five-year service combine to ensure that an apprentice

---

[1] 'There can be little doubt that . . . the requirement of a seven-year term', laid down in the Statute of Artificers of 1563, was then already widely applied on a voluntary basis.' Margaret Gay Davies, *The Enforcement of English Apprenticeship 1563-1642*, p.10. Harvard University Press (1956).

[2] *Apprenticeship 1925-26*, p. 80.

[3] In corporate towns, the minimum age was 24 years.

completes his term not later than at the age of 21 years.[1] This regulation is in line with the general wage structure which accords adult rates of pay to workers on reaching the age of 21. There is, moreover,

'the legal character of the relationship which makes its termination at the age of 21 years desirable, since on the attainment of that age it is open to the apprentice to repudiate the contract.'[2]

However, considerations other than legal render it today anything but desirable to make 21 years the upper age limit for apprenticeship.

In previous pages, we have repeatedly dwelt on the stress to which the old institution of apprenticeship has been subjected by continual technological change and vice versa. But the change has not merely been a steady one; the rate of change has greatly increased. As automation is beginning to gather momentum, occupational mobility of labour is becoming increasingly important. Jobs becoming redundant through automation will make it necessary for many adult workers to retrain for other jobs. Under the present apprenticeship regulations, however, such retraining is blocked by rigid age limits for the beginning and completion of apprenticeship and by the stipulation of a five-year term of service. The regulations by which apprenticeship must be completed by the age of 21 years or thereabouts deny a retraining to, and thereby endanger the future employment of, those whose jobs become redundant; this is particularly serious in view of the ageing of the population.

The lifting of the ban on apprenticeship for adults is thus a necessary means for securing occupational and industrial mobility of labour in adjustment to economic and technical changes. Naturally, some difficulties will have to be overcome. Wage arrangements for apprentices over 21 years pose the problem of how to reconcile a lower-than-skilled rate with sufficiency of earning for a man and his family; but the urgency of facilitating the training and retraining of adults is such that a solution must be found. The difficulty is lessened if the

[1] An exception is made for apprenticeship interrupted by National Service.
[2] *Apprenticeship 1925-26*, p. 83.

duration of apprenticeship is curtailed; five years are widely recognised to be an unnecessarily long term even for juvenile apprentices: adult persons, provided they have had a good basic education, should, because of their maturity and experience, require a considerably shorter period of training in the specific skill required in a new job. Neither in the U.S.A. nor in Western Germany is there an age limit for apprenticeship, nor is the term of service in those countries as long as it is at present in Great Britain.[1]

THE 'SKILLED TICKET'

The division of functions in the recognition of an apprentice as a skilled craftsman is remarkable. The training which makes an apprentice eligible for the skilled ticket is given by a firm. After five years' satisfactory service, the employer endorses the indentures and hands them to the apprentice. The endorsement does not attest the apprentice's competence in his trade. The union does not concern itself with the adequacy of the training but accepts the endorsed indenture as sufficient for issuing to the ex-apprentice the 'skilled ticket' which entitles a worker to the wage rate of a craftsman.

What guarantee of the new craftsman's proficiency does this procedure give? In principle there are two different ways in which the candidate for a job can satisfy a would-be employer that he is qualified to do it. One is, by having been with a trainer who is known to give good training; the other is to have proved his expertness in tests and/or examinations.

Today, neither way is taken. A craft apprentice does not have to prove his proficiency in order to be recognised as a skilled worker; his apprenticeship is successfully completed when he has served the stipulated time 'to the satisfaction of his

[1] For the U.S.A., see *The National Apprenticeship Program*', U.S. Department of Labor, Bureau of Apprenticeship, 1953 edition, p. 7 ; more details in *The Mobility of Tool and Die Makers 1940-1951*; Bulletin No. 1120, U.S. Department of Labor, and Bulletins Nos. 1150 and 1162 for other 'critical' occupations; further, *Letterpress Printing*, Productivity Team Report, para. 98; for Germany, see *Gaining Skill: A report of an investigation of industrial apprentices in Western Germany*', p. 18. Birmingham Productivity Association (1955).

employer'. Hence, everything turns upon the employer's capacity and willingness to train apprentices. It is therefore a matter of grave concern that, by and large, employers need no qualification for taking on apprentices; that no supervision and control exist to ensure that employers are not only qualified to train but that they are actually training their apprentices to proper standards; and that minimum requirements as to amount or length of training are not enforced, or laid down.

THE VALUE OF THE INDENTURE

The endeavour to secure minimum training standards has no doubt been a major cause of the sustained (and not unsuccessful) official drive for the formal indenture of apprentices. In practice, indenture fails to answer that purpose, for it leaves the quantity and quality of training at the discretion of the employers of apprentices. The training given by employers may fall short in two different ways: masters may be inadequate to the task, or they may decide to give only part of a broad and thorough training. The first is to be found in smaller shops—since the repeal of the Statute of Artificers in 1814, anybody can become a master of apprentices, at any rate in the engineering trades; and no minimum standards are laid down as to the equipment of a factory in which apprentices are to be trained. The second case is that of large well-staffed and well-equipped firms where good training is given for an initial period but discontinued—in some cases after a few months, in others after a year or two, but nearly always well before half of the apprenticeship period is over; the result is that narrowly specialised or even one-skill men are produced instead of versatile craftsmen. Safeguards against this decay of craft training would be either the enforcement of minimum standards not only for the employers' training capacity but also for actual training performance, or else a testing of the apprentices' proficiency before they are recognised as skilled workers.

The value of the indenture varies between different industries and from different points of view. In a schematic way, the situation may be put thus :—

COMPLETION OF APPRENTICESHIP

THE VALUE OF THE INDENTURE is

as a guarantee of good training :—nil ;

as a contract of employment for five years :—

in Printing	}	under full employment, greater to em-
„ Engineering		ployers than to apprentices ;
„ Building		because of business fluctuations, negative to employers ;

as a precondition of obtaining craftsman's work :—

in Printing   paramount
„ Engineering   varied[1]
„ Building   at present, not great ;

as a promise of life-long security of employment :—

in Printing	great ; but threat of British printing industry being by-passed : (*a*) office machines ; (*b*) overseas printing firms ;[2]
„ Engineering	issue not arising during full employment; but trusted by craftsmen and by parents of
„ Building	(potential) apprentices to become important in a recession.

THE VALUE OF TECHNICAL-EDUCATION CERTIFICATES

It seems in place here to reflect in a similar way on the value of the certificates attesting success in a technical examination. An assessment of the intrinsic usefulness of technical education to craftsmen's and technicians' productive work is outside the scope of this study: we are concerned with the value of these 'paper qualifications' for the certificate holder's earning power and chances of promotion.

The C. & G. certificates do not bring financial rewards; they may or may not help the holder to get promotion, but at present there are many foremen who have not got a certificate (this helps to explain, incidentally, why so many apprentices feel that their superiors discourage them in their technical studies). However, as technical education of apprentices at

---

[1] Mr. V. L. Allen lists pattern makers, sheet-metal workers, coppersmiths and heating and ventilating engineers as the few engineering trades in which a skilled ticket is required for finding a job. *Power in Trade Unions*, p.45 (1954) 'Engineering' here excludes shipbuilding—this explains the absence of boilermakers from the list.   [2] See pp. 167f and 170.

large is getting more firmly established, the passing of an examination might become a prerequisite of promotion.

The advantages of holding an O.N.C. must be examined separately for craft apprentices and for Engineering apprentices. For craft apprentices, the direct financial reward is not great[1]: the prizes which firms may give for a successful examination are no worth-while reward for years of study, including evening classes and homework; an increase in pay, i.e. a higher rate for holding the O.N.C., is more acceptable to apprentices, but it ceases when their time is up, because the trade unions' wage policy does not allow a higher wage rate than the district rate.[2] Non-financial rewards are more important, namely the promise or prospect of promotion to staff status. But the craftsman has no certainty that the O.N.C. will better his position.

For those apprentices who set their target high, the O.N.C. is the platform from which they start the Advanced course leading to the H.N.C. For the less ambitious, the O.N.C. is a goal in itself. In firms with apprenticeship grading, a pass in the O.N.C. examination is expected from Engineering apprentices; in some of these firms, an Engineering apprentice who fails to obtain the O.N.C., becomes a craftsman after his five years' service, not a technician; in some other firms, he becomes, but also remains, a 'junior technician.' In firms without formal grading, ex-craft apprentices may become technicians, and those who hold, or subsequently obtain, the O.N.C. may or may not find it an advantage for promotion. (One employer stated that a brilliant technical-college student was not necessarily good at technicians' work).

In many cases, therefore, the O.N.C. gives chances but no promise of reward to its holder: neither does it carry the claim to a higher rate of pay (as the comparable certificate does for Medical Laboratory Technicians), nor is it the official or customary prerequisite for specified semi-professional occupations or grades. Among holders of the O.N.C. there seems to be considerable dissatisfaction with the small effect it has on their promotion and remuneration.

[1] See James Brown, 'The Apprentice Engineer and Incentives to Study' in *Vocational Aspect*, Autumn 1952, p.108-113.
[2] See p. 172 below on discouragement of skill.

In spite of this, the O.N.C. is coveted because of its prestige and of its 'sales value.' Firms advertising for technicians or 'intermediate engineers' often list the O.N.C. as a required qualification. The O.N.C. attests not only a certain standard of technical and theoretical knowledge, but also the sustained effort and discipline of several years' part-time study (only a small minority of O.N.C.'s are obtained by full-time students).

IX

TRADE UNIONS AND APPRENTICESHIP

WHEN discussing trade-union attitude to apprenticeship, we must not forget that over a large part of industry apprenticeship is not an issue at all (except for a relatively small number of maintenance men). There is no apprenticeship in mining, textiles, boot and shoe manufacture or railway transport, for instance.

In those industries in which apprenticeship exists, the trade unions' attitude to it differs according to the grade of worker they organise. Craft unions have a paramount positive interest in apprenticeship, as it is the foundation of their members' superior status; by contrast, unions catering for non-skilled workers in these industries cannot be well disposed to the apprenticeship system, since the privileges of apprenticed craftsmen are maintained at the expense of less-skilled workers.

In the printing industry, a clear division between craft and other unions prevails: the Typographical Association (T.A.) is the largest of several pure craft unions, while the National Amalgamated Trade Society of Operative Printers and Assistants (N.A.T.S.O.P.A.) organises non-skilled workers.[1]

The grouping of trade unions is similar in the building industry; there are separate craft unions for the several apprenticeable trades, including bricklaying and plastering, whereas building labourers join one of the general trade unions. In practice, however, many building workers become members of the craft unions without having served their apprenticeship[2].

[1] The bookbinders and machine rulers do not form a craft union of their own, but they constitute a craft section of an otherwise non-craft union, the National Union of Printing, Bookbinding and Paper Workers.

[2] See p. 168f, below.

TRADE UNIONS AND APPRENTICESHIP

Some pure craft unions are extant also in the engineering and allied industries, among them the United Society of Boilermakers. But these are comparatively small. The biggest unions—the Amalgamated Engineering Union and the Electrical Trades Union— have ceased to be craft unions, since they admit to membership non-skilled as well as skilled workers. These unions therefore represent groups with divergent interests in apprenticeship, and their apprenticeship policy is complex, partly undivulged and not easy to interpret.[1]

This type of union is growing in importance, while pure craft unionism is on the decline. But craft unions have been the breeding-place for apprenticeship as we know it today, and the young multi-grade unions retain many features characteristic of craft unions; the A.E.U. and the E.T.U. each have a special section reserved for skilled workers. In view of this situation, the following exposition is focused on craft unions, understood in a wide sense so as to cover craft sections; this leads on to the discussion of the role of apprenticeship in a multi-grade union with a craft legacy, exemplified by the A.E.U., the largest union of this type.

Trade unions are not parties to indentures. Apprenticeship, just as other contracts of employment, is a contract between an individual employer and an individual apprentice (and his guardian).[2] The trade unions' great influence on the apprenticeship system is exercised through a multiplicity of arrangements: the trade unions are parties to semi-official National Schemes and to National Agreements with employers' organisations; to district, local and single-firm agreements; they have a hand in 'trade practices', 'existing customs' and

[1] These former craft unions which now admit members of all grades of skill have been described as ' "diluted" craft unions' (G. D. H. Cole, *Introduction to Trade Unionism*, 1953, p.81) and as 'semi-craft unions' (B. C. Roberts, *Trade Union Government and Administration in Great Britain*, p.492). But neither term seems quite satisfactory. ' Diluted' is ambiguous because it refers here to trade union membership to which less-skilled workers of all grades are admitted, not only 'dilutees', i.e. upgraded semi-skilled operatives. 'Semi-craft union' is ambiguous because of the similarity of the terms 'semi-craft' and 'semi-skilled', when in fact skilled as well as semi-skilled and also unskilled workers are members of these unions.

[2] In the building industry a representative of the employers' side of the local Joint Apprenticeship Committee is an additional party to the indenture—see above, p. 31.

'understandings'; they make rules and regulations which may or may not be recognised by the employers' association concerned, and they follow procedures, e.g. in issuing the skilled ticket, which are not codified or published. However, this bewildering motley of regulations will be shown to be the expression of a method built up with a purpose.

HISTORICAL BACKGROUND

There is twofold reason why trade union attitude to apprenticeship has to be considered against a historical background. Firstly, the apprenticeship system, which has been a corner-stone of trade-union policy for nearly 150 years, is still, as the Webbs found it 'in form and in purpose practically identical with that which prevailed long before Trade Unionism was heard of.'[1] Secondly, the methods of the trade unions' present apprenticeship policy (and indeed of trade-union policy in general) are in kind, if not in their relative importance, the same as they were a century ago.

The main purpose to which the apprenticeship system is being put by the unions is regulation of entry into skilled occupations; the form consists of various provisions which will be discussed presently; and the method, although collective bargaining has been gaining much ground, still contains a substantial admixture of autonomous trade-union regulation.

Restriction of entry into occupations has been a major function of the apprenticeship system since the days of the guilds. Journeymen craftsmen had been among the beneficiaries of statutory apprenticeship. The number of apprentices had been limited and common law had supported the craftsmen's claim to their exclusive right to their trades (hence the term 'illegal men.')

In the first quarter of the 19th century, two pieces of legislation profoundly affected the legal position of the craftsmen, one to their detriment, the other to their advantage. The Apprentices Act of 1814 abolished statutory apprenticeship, that is to say, trades were no longer closed to unapprenticed

[1] *Industrial Democracy*, p.454.

men. The Combination Laws Repeal Acts of 1824 and 1825, on the other hand, strengthened the workers' position by making trade unions lawful; and since non-skilled labour remained unorganised for more than another half century, it was the craftsmen who benefited from the freedom to combine.

To the dispassionate student today, the repeal of the anti-combination Acts appears as the logical and equitable complement of the repeal of statutory apprenticeship: the State, after relinquishing the legislative regulation of entry into occupations and the support of craftsmen's exclusive right to their trade, was induced to make lawful the combination of workers for taking care of their own interests. Concomitantly, therefore, the Acts of 1814 and of 1824/25 opened the way for collective bargaining—in theory.

The actual course of events was not that smooth. The legal 'trade-union emancipation' (effected ten years after the abrogation of State regulation) was not generally accompanied by concurrence on the part of the employers. In important industries, including the iron trades, employers were not ready to recognise the trade unions' right to negotiate on behalf of their members. The trade unions had to fight their way.

The only unions then in existence were craft unions. Their aim was to restore the old order under which, at least nominally, trades had been closed to unapprenticed men. Their method was decided for them by the State's laissez faire attitude and by the employers' repudiation. Left to fend for themselves and being refused negotiation, trade unions resorted to what is now called the method of autonomous regulation.[1] 'This term,' Mr. J. D. M. Bell defines, 'would include any way of regulating (or attempting to regulate) working conditions by the enforcement of the unions' own rules and internal administrative arrangements.'[2] The concept 'autonomous regulation' covers therefore the laying down of rules which a trade union is yet unable to enforce in a collective agreement. They are enforced, to a greater or less degree, by the actions of trade-union members in the workplace, by their refusal to work except in accordance

---

[1] 'British industrial relations have, in the main, developed by way of industrial autonomy.' (O. Kahn-Freund, 'Legal Framework' in Flanders & Clegg, *op. cit.*, p. 44.   [2] 'Trade Unions', ibid., p. 192.

with the rules. The degree of enforcement varies from time to time and from place to place, in accordance with the relative economic strength of the employers and of the union.

As trade unions grew stronger, employers accepted the principle of collective bargaining. Wages and conditions of work became subjects of collective agreements; and 'procedural agreements' came to be concluded on provisions for avoiding disputes. By contrast, negotiation on questions concerning apprentices, and their manpower policy in general, was persistently resisted by the employers. In 1898, the Amalgamated Society of Engineers had formally to acknowledge the employers' right to 'select, train and employ those they considered best adapted to the various operations and to pay them according to their ability as workmen.'[1] In 1922, this was replaced by the equivocal, not yet superseded clause: 'The employers have the right to manage their establishments and the trade unions have the right to exercise their functions.'[2]

It was not before December 1937 that the A.E.U. and other Engineering Unions gained the employers' consent to negotiate on behalf of junior male workers; and apprentices benefit from the agreement only indirectly:

'Apprentices serving under Indentures or written Agreements between the employers and the parents or guardians are not covered by this Agreement but the [employers'] Federation undertakes to recommend its members to apply to such apprentices conditions not less favourable than those conceded to other apprentices by settlements made under the machinery of this Agreement.'[3]

Even now it is a contested issue how far questions related to apprenticeship are a purely managerial function, how far a subject for collective bargaining.

METHOD OF TRADE UNIONS' APPRENTICESHIP POLICY

Trade unions still attempt to settle issues connected with apprenticeship by way of autonomous regulation. This method

---

[1] Terms of Settlement, quote by J. B. Jefferys, *The Story of the Engineers*, 1800-1945, p.151.

[2] Agreement on Procedure for Avoiding Disputes, Clause 1(a).

[3] Confederation of Shipbuilding and Engineering Unions, Handbook of National Agreements, 1949, p.183.

is being applied not only to matters whose acknowledgment as objects of collective bargaining is in dispute. Quite generally, trade unions have maintained the procedure of their militant days of making autonomous stipulations in order to soften the employers' resistance. Although collective bargaining has come to be the predominant method, unions continue to prepare for future negotiation by autonomous regulation.[1] Moreover, while a national or district agreement may be unobtainable, one firm or other may concede a union's terms and come to an informal 'understanding'; in course of time, the terms may become recognised as 'existing practices.' In other words, by autonomous regulation trade unions bring pressure to bear on individual firms and on employers' associations at all levels.

Illustrations of such informal pressure can be obtained by a perusal of the Ministry of Labour's Report on Apprenticeship in 1925-26. In the text of Volume VI it is stated that

'except in a few specialised branches there are no agreements between employers and workpeople determining the conditions of employment of apprentices in the engineering industry. . . .

'The Amalgamated Engineering Union . . . has no rules affecting the conditions of employment of apprentices. Indeed . . . the [employers'] Federation states that they "do not admit the right of any trade union to regulate the wages and conditions of apprentices."[2]

In the appendix to the same volume, however, an Analysis of Trade Union Rules and Regulations shows the A.E.U. as having stipulations on length and on ages of commencement and termination of apprenticeship; these are marked 'C' which indicates 'conditions reported by trade unions to be customary

---

[1] This point needs to be stressed, because writers at the present time are liable to understate the persisting importance of the method of autonomous regulation; Mr. Flanders, e.g., emphasises 'the significant continuity in the transition from union regulation to collective agreement', adding only that the transition was not always smooth or complete. 'Collective Bargaining', in Flanders and Clegg, *op. cit.*, p. 265. The issue is, however, stated in plain words in G.D.H. Cole, *An Introduction to Trade Unionism*, 1953 edition, p. 17: 'This way of enforcing minimum conditions of employment without formal agreement . . . is still important in many occupations today. This informal kind of pressure . . .'

[2] Vol. VI, p.42ff.

though not contained in any rule or regulation known to the [Ministry].'[1]

Whether, and if so when, a trade union's terms become embodied in an agreement depends on the relative strength of the employers and the trade union involved and also on the state of the labour market in general. In times of full employment, employers may feel bound to comply with autonomous trade-union regulations which they may hope to disregard under conditions of less full employment.

It is this continual diffuse struggle for control of apprenticeship, with various issues at various firms and localities differently positioned between autonomous regulation and collective agreement, which accounts for the heterogeneity of the present body of apprenticeship regulations in some industries, particularly in Engineering. This is in significant contrast to Printing, where, for the time being anyhow, the craft unions are in virtual control of apprenticeship regulation and where accordingly nearly all terms of the unions are incorporated in the industry's tidy and comprehensive National Scheme for apprenticeship.

OBJECTS OF TRADE UNIONS' APPRENTICESHIP POLICY

The circumstances attending the union membership of apprentices show in a nutshell the complexity of trade unions' apprenticeship policy. Under the Trade Union Act of 1876 the minimum age for membership of a trade union is 16 years.[2] As long as apprenticeship generally began at an earlier age, the younger apprentices were thus precluded from union membership. (This still applies to those printing and building apprentices who begin their apprenticeship at 15). But trade unions have been able to enroll youngsters as 'juveniles' or 'associates'; the Amalgamated Engineering Union e.g. admits boys from 15 years onward as members. Until not so long ago, apprentices in some industries were 'forbidden by the terms of their

---

[1] ibid, p. 171ff; see also Upgrading of Foundry Personnel, p. 164 below.

[2] The legal position is not entirely clear; see B. C. Roberts, *op. cit.* p.37, note 1.

indentures from becoming members of trade unions for industrial purposes'[1] during the whole period of their service. However, trade unions themselves were by no means keen to enlist apprentices before they had served for four or five years and were 18 or 19 years old.[2] Even today, the drive for '100% trade-union organisation' does not extend to apprentices.

How can the trade unions' indifference towards membership of apprentices be reconciled with the unions' deep concern in apprenticeship? The answer is that craft unions' apprenticeship policy is activated by conflicting motives. From a craft union's point of view, apprentices figure in a dual role. On the one hand, they are the rising generation of its members on whom the union's future depends—this explains the craft unions' urgent concern in the apprenticeship system. On the other hand, apprentices are a threat to the craftsmen's 'right to the job' and to their bargaining power in wage negotiations: as cheap labour during apprenticehood, and as potential cause of 'overstocking the trade' when they become craftsmen themselves. In the conditions of the 19th century, craftsmen were for these reasons often bitterly antagonistic to apprentices, and this explains the craft unions' lack of enthusiasm, to say the least, for union membership of apprentices. In recent decades, the antagonism has, on the whole, abated. For a variety of reasons—mainly the adoption of a full-employment policy, the long-term decline of the birthrate, and the reduced eagerness of employers as a whole to take on apprentices—the threat to craftsmen from apprentices has become less important than that from dilutees. However, craftsmen's feelings similar to those prevalent in the 19th century are not unknown today. Thus, in discussions of the method to lessen the acute shortage of printers after the last war, some full members of the Typographical Association preferred [dilution][3] to a larger intake of apprentices who would become regular journeymen.[4]

[1] Memorandum of Ministry of Labour, in *Factors in Industrial and Commercial Efficiency* (Balfour Report), p.147 (1927).

[2] Appendix C. of the Ministry of Labour's Report on Apprenticeship, 1925-26, Vol. VI.

[3] See p. 163 below on the stipulation that in a trade recession dilutees are to make way for apprenticed men.

[4] A. E. Musson, *The Typographical Association*, p.429 (1954).

TRADE UNIONS AND APPRENTICESHIP

The proportion of apprentices who have actually joined a trade union is not known. Unions vary in their efforts to enlist apprentices as members and to interest them in Union affairs. Indifference in this respect may be a direct legacy of past hostility, or it may be explained on more general grounds; as Professor Cole observes, 'the weakest spot of the Trade Union movement is its relatively scanty provision for the adolescent worker. . . . Most Trade Unions are in spirit adult bodies and do not accommodate themselves too easily to the ways of youth.'[1] The two explanations are not necessarily unconnected: may not the adult workers' old fear of cheap apprentice labour or boy labour lie at the root of the trade unions' attitude?

Trade unions' *interests* in apprenticeship fall under three headings: apprentices' wages and conditions of work; apprentice training; and regulation of entry into trades. Trade-union concern under the first two headings pertains to one or other aspect of the apprentices' welfare; the third interest, and the dominant one, pertains to the strengthening of the adult craftsman's position, apprenticeship being used as a means to that end.

CONDITIONS OF WORK AND WAGE RATES OF APPRENTICES

These are now regulated by general National Agreements between the two sides of various industries. In engineering, as already mentioned, the employers fell in with this long-standing demand of the unions as late as 1937. A few years later, during the war, the engineering unions secured better terms of pay for apprentices. They are now paid the same time rates as other boys and youths of their age; the rate is expressed as a proportion of the district rate of the adult fitter, rising from $27\frac{1}{2}\%$ at 16 to $62\frac{1}{2}\%$ at 20 years of age.[2] In total earnings, however, the apprentice lags behind, because he receives little, if any, piece wages. In printing, the apprentices' wages are similarly based

---

[1] *Introduction to Trade Unionism*, p. 75.

[2] The latter percentage ($62\frac{1}{2}$) for the last year of apprenticeship compares with about 34% in 1909 and 44% in 1925 (*Apprenticeship 1925-26*).

on the rates for journeymen (but the rates are different in the various printing trades); they rise to 60% in the last year of apprenticeship. Rates for male learners of semi-skilled printing occupations (not members of the craft unions) are negotiated in terms of shillings per week; the amount is about the same as the pay of apprentices of their age but constitutes, at the age of 20, approximately 70% of the minimum adult rate in the learner's trade.[1] In the building industry, apprentices (until they are 20) earn considerably less than labourers of the same age, even where they partake in an incentive wage scheme.

APPRENTICE TRAINING

Trade-union interest is alert and active in various spheres of education. We would mention here that the Education Committee of the Trades Union Congress 'would like to see the extension of day release to the much larger number of young workers who are not apprentices or trainees'.[2] But apprentice training is not one of these spheres: craft-union interest in apprentices' learning their trade is rather limp. (An apparent exception, in the printing trades, will presently be shown actually to re-inforce this general verdict). How little store craft unions today set by good training is evinced in many ways. They do not ask for a proof of competence before issuing the 'skilled ticket' to an apprentice who has completed his term of bound service. The unions have been indifferent to the fact that since 1814 an employer is not required to have a qualification for taking on apprentices. While trade-union representatives co-operate in joint apprenticeship bodies where these exist[3]—the engineering industry has no local joint apprenticeship committees in S.W. England, and the regional committee meets not even once a year—there is here none of the keenness which characterizes trade-union interest in other matters concerning apprentices. Furthermore, far from claiming a larger share in the control of training, unions are not found

[1] British Federation of Master Printers, *Basic Wages and Conditions*, E. & W. (except London), February, 1954.

[2] *T.U.C. Report, 1956*, p. 171.

[3] In the Survey area, among the three industries under review this co-operation is most developed in Building.

154

protesting against training being taken out of their members' hands by the spreading habit of firms of removing apprentice training from the shopfloor. Finally, trade unions have by no means been a driving force in the development of technical education for apprentices.

There can be no doubt about the present unconcern of craft unions in apprentice training. For whatever ultimate reasons craft unions may have at one time been interested in apprentice training, they have long since accepted the progressive de-skilling of the crafts as an inevitable implication of technical progress, much as they may deplore the disintegration of craftsmanship and its accompaniment, the influx into their trades of unapprenticed workers. 'And once a trade union has failed to limit the entry into its trade then it very soon loses interest in educational standards.'[1] On the face of it, this explanation seems to be corroborated *e contrario* by the state of affairs in the printing industry. There, the craft unions have secured their members' prerogative to printing jobs; for compositors anyhow, the unions watch closely over the observance of the training syllabuses laid down by the industry's Apprenticeship Authority. Actually, however, the training is not determined by the requirements of modern mechanised type setting, but devised so as to retard technical progress in the industry (see p.104). In other words, the printing craft unions' real concern is not apprentice training but the underpinning of the monopolistic position of apprenticed craftsmen.

REGULATION OF ENTRY INTO SKILLED OCCUPATIONS

In the post-war literature on trade unionism, most authors make light of restrictive practices in general and of restriction of numbers in particular. It is true that restriction of entry in the narrowest sense is on the wane: limitation of the number of apprentices, as imposed by a system of ratios of apprentices to journeymen in the printing trades, has become an exception. However, if the term 'regulation of entry' is given its full meaning, the result is a rather different assessment of the

---

[1] V. L. Allen, *op. cit.*, p.45, adapting a statement of the Webbs to modern conditions.

situation. Trade unions effect or attempt regulation of entry into their trades by a whole series of restrictive provisions, quite apart from the exclusion of women from many skilled trades. Provisions for regulating entry in the wider sense fall into three groups :—
1. Limitation of apprentices.
2. Restraint of the flow of apprentices
    (a) long-term service
    (b) rigid age limits for beginning and completion of apprenticeship.
3. Closing the trade to outsiders
    (a) to craftsmen of other trades (demarcation)
    (b) to unapprenticed workers (anti-dilutionism).

All these restrictive measures relate to, or are based on, apprenticeship; most of them were taken over by the trade unions from the previous regime of statutory apprenticeship.

1. Limitatian of Apprentices

Since apprenticeship is the normal gate of entry into the skilled occupations, limitation of apprentices is the most obvious manner of regulating entry into these trades. It is, however, not effective unless entry of adult outsiders (and of boy labour) is prevented. Under the Tudor Statute of Artificers, limitation of apprentices was therefore accompanied by disallowance of the employment of unapprenticed men in skilled trades;[1] and today, the imposition of apprentice ratios in the printing trades is accompanied by demarcation and non-dilution.

But most trade unions do not now press seriously for this provision. In Engineering and in Building where limitation of apprentices prevails little if at all, this situation has been reached from different directions.

The Amalgamated Engineering Union has formally renounced, although not without a reservation, the fixing of apprentice ratios:

'The proportion of apprentices to journeymen . . . shall not be subject to specific determination. This shall be without prejudice

---

[1] The journeymen's fights and petitions, in the 18th century, against the intrusion into their trades by 'illegal men' show that the latter provision was increasingly disobeyed, but this is irrelevant here.

to the freedom which the Unions have to raise under the Provisions for Avoiding Disputes questions affecting the employment, or interest of adult workpeople.' (1943 Agreement.)

In the post-war period of full employment, there has not been much occasion to make use of the clause of reservation, but sometimes a firm's apprentice-farming tendencies are curbed by trade-union remonstration.

In building, on the other hand, a maximum apprentice ratio was agreed, in this case with a qualifying clause providing for increasing the ratio:

'The normal proportion is 1 apprentice to 4 journeymen although variations in this proportion may in present circumstances be mutually agreed between employers' and workpeople's representatives' (National Scheme, 1947).

In 1953 the clause was deleted, and no ratio is now laid down.

Limitation of apprentices has, with certain exceptions, ceased to be a prominent issue. This does not mean, however, that the struggle of regulation for entry has ended; it rather means that the war is now being fought on other fronts.

2. Restraint of the flow of Apprentices

While yielding ground in the matter of limitation of apprentices, trade unions have so far been adamant regarding the restraint of the flow of apprentices which is effected by (a) long duration of, and (b) age limits for, apprenticeship.

(a) The stipulation of a five-year apprenticeship restricts entry into trades, to some extent directly but in the main indirectly. The long duration of apprenticeship at comparatively low earnings must act as a disincentive; however, there are, in the survey area in any case, more recruits than openings for apprenticeship. Boys are willing—and their parents support them—to undergo what has been called the endurance test of apprenticeship, because it gains them the privileged position of craftsmen. This brings us to the less manifest bearing of protracted apprenticeship on the regulation of entry. For it is in virtue of their long years of bound service (rather than of superior skill) that craftsmen claim differential wages and the exclusive right to their trades. The latter prerogative, however, means barring the entry of others and a restriction of the supply of labour. It is true that this kind of injustice suffered by unapprenticed workers has become much less wide-spread. Today, so many good, well-paid manual jobs are obtainable other than by way of apprenticeship that personal injustice to individuals by the exclusiveness of the apprenticeship system is no longer so serious, especially not in large labour markets.

However, the industries in which apprenticeship prevails are important ones, and the insistence on prolonged apprenticeship, to be served at a rigidly fixed age, not only blocks the flow of labour into skilled occupations, but has harmful repercussions over a much wider field.[1]

(b) As we have discussed in the preceding chapter, completion of apprenticeship at the age of 21 is the lodestar by which duration of, and age of entry into, apprenticeship are determined. Age limits were laid down in trade-union rules and regulations long before being incorporated in agreements with employers and in National Schemes. The stand on termination of apprenticeship at 21 years of age, together with the requirement of a five-year term, makes 16 years the maximum age of entry (even where not specifically laid down). This has adverse effects of two different kinds. First, it keeps out boys who want to stay at school in order to pass an examination or who find that the original choice of their life's work was not the right one; relief of this sort of irritation is now under consideration (see the Carr Report) and there seems to be a fair chance of success. By contrast, nothing is yet being done regarding the second, bigger matter, namely the exclusion from apprenticeship of persons over 21.

3. Closing the Trade to Outsiders

Measures regulating number and flow of apprentices are evidently of no avail unless the entry of outsiders into the trade is also regulated. Skill acquired by apprenticeship in a specific craft has never by itself sufficed to reserve the various trades to the craftsmen apprenticed in them, and modern technical development has sharply accentuated this insufficiency. With

[1] See p. 171.

increasing mechanisation, craft unions have found the question of how to control the entry of outsiders into their trades an increasingly difficult one. The challenge comes from two sides: craftsmen of other trades and unapprenticed workers. The device for preventing the interchange of different trades[1] is termed demarcation in current usage. For the measures taken to defend craftsmen's jobs against unapprenticed workers no term has yet been coined; they may be described as anti-dilutionism or as vertical demarcation.

The craft unions' struggles to enforce demarcation and non-dilution have had different success in the several industries, with different implications for apprenticeship. The most important development in this respect has been the transformation of the powerful craft unions in the engineering and allied industries.

Engineering
Some pure craft unions survive in the engineering and allied industries; their uncompromising insistence on demarcation and non-dilution is similar to the policy of the printers' unions; but since these practices are opposed by the engineering employers, they are pursued by way of autonomous regulation.

Of greater consequence for the future is the complex demarcation and control-of-dilution policy of the big trade unions which are now multi-grade unions but retain strong elements of craft unionism. The following discussion is based on the policy of the oldest and largest of them, the Amalgamated Engineering Union.

Faced with a rapid expansion of the engineering industry and with continual technical progress involving ever-increasing mechanisation, the A.E.U. and its predecessors have never been able to secure craftsmen the exclusive right to their traditional jobs. In some periods the competition of rival craftsmen has been the more serious challenge, in others, that of non-skilled workers.

The A.E.U.'s policy in respect to both, demarcation and

---

[1] Demarcation between non-skilled occupations, as that between the porters at Covent Garden Market, is comparatively rare.

non-dilution, has been affected by changes in trade-union organisation. Through amalgamation and federation of rival unions, demarcation struggles are turned from inter-union into intra-union issues; similarly, admission to membership of non-craftsmen means that the A.E.U.'s policy as to dilution has now to reconcile the interests of rival groups among its own members.

(a) *Demarcation.* Demarcation in Engineering is less formalised than in Printing and in Building; nevertheless, demarcation is interlocked with the apprentice training given by employers. The National Scheme for apprenticeship in the engineering industry does not give a list of apprenticeable trades, and demarcation is not generally introduced from the start, except in such trades as boiler-makers and sheet metal workers which are represented by pure craft unions. Apprentices are often indentured as 'turner and fitter' or for 'general engineering'.[1] In some smaller firms, this foreshadows a not very thorough training of such variety as the firm's range of work and of machines provides. More often, however, the non-specification of the trade to be learnt foreshadows 'specialisation' at an early stage of the apprenticeship—a euphemism for training in a narrow range of jobs or even a one-skill job. A firm's assertion that apprentices specialise in the trade of their choice is not always convincing, to put it mildly; apprentices feel strongly about this.

Once the apprentice is freed and issued with a skilled ticket, he is subject to the demarcation between crafts. Lines and stringency of demarcation are determined by existing practices and vary between districts and between firms; details are not published.

Through the amalgamation of different craft unions in the A.E.U., the number of open demarcation disputes has diminished—rival claims are now settled behind closed doors within the big union. Fewer working days may thereby be lost through strikes, but as far as demarcation puts barriers between types of work which by objective standards are

---

[1] Quite large firms may be found to indenture all their craft apprentices for the various engineering trades as instrument makers ; or all as tool makers.

interchangeable[1], it hampers the utilisation of craftsmen and thus restricts the supply of labour in the skilled occupations.

(*b*) *Control of Dilution:* The employment in engineering trades of unapprenticed men has been a major issue between employers and craft unions from the early days of the unions onward. The engineering unions have been fighting a prolonged rearguard action in this respect. Their original claim that all machines should be manned by craftsmen has long since been relinquished. The development in the engineering industry— enormous growth, ever-increasing specialisation, introduction of more and more automatic machines—has brought into the engineering shops masses of non-craftsmen who are paid less than skilled rates.

A large new 'class' of semi-skilled workers has arisen. Between 1914 and 1933 alone, the approximate proportion of semi-skilled workers in Engineering rose from 20% to 57%, and that of craftsmen dropped correspondingly, with little change in the proportion of unskilled labourers.[2] Apart from the lower rate of pay, semi-skilled workers have the further advantage for the employer that he can deploy them according to the requirements of the work in hand: they are subject neither to demarcation nor to fixed wage rates.

This is not the place to deal with the phases of the craftsmen's retreat or with the effects which progressive mechanisation had and continues to have on craftsmanship and on apprenticeship. It seems sufficient here to distinguish two broad categories of jobs into which non-craftsmen have entered, viz. jobs manifestly below a craftsman's skill, and jobs still claimed as 'skilled men's work.'

The first case does not present a serious problem of regulation of entry. In a rapidly expanding industry, craftsmen could not and would not maintain a claim to the simpler, repetitive jobs

---

[1] 'Work which is not an essential and distinctive part of the work of any one class [of worker], although it may be incidental or ancillary to one or more crafts, may be performed by anyone who is competent to do it' was a recommendation on Interchangeability in the Report of Joint Inquiry into Foreign Competition and Conditions in the Shipbuilding Industry, 1926. Quoted from *Are Trade Unions Obstructive? An Impartial Inquiry.* Joint Editors John Hilton, J. J. Mallon and others (1935) p.287.

[2] For sources of these estimates, see K. G. J. C. Knowles, *Strikes*, p.172, footnote 6.

which came to be acknowledged as semi-skilled work. In regard to these jobs, there is no restriction of numbers on the part of the A.E.U. or other trade unions. By contrast, entry into jobs of the second category, on the ever changing border-line of 'skilled men's work' is now to a considerable extent subject to regulation by the unions. This has come about in the following way.

From the beginning of this century, the craftsmen's position as to the manning of machines 'turning out skilled work' became increasingly undermined. This 'machine question' remained intractable for decades, although the dilution schemes introduced during the first World War suggested a solution: in 1915, the craft unions waived temporarily the prerogative to jobs which were customarily theirs,[1] but employers had to pay 'the rate for the job' to dilutees who were upgraded to perform skilled men's work. After the restoration of pre-war practices, the Amalgamated Society of Engineers (the predecessor of the A.E.U.) tried to fall back on the war-time compromise for solving the 'machine question.' In 1920, the union proposed to the employers that all machines should be graded and some of them, e.g. capstan, combination and turret lathes, should carry the full rate for fitters and turners, irrespective of the training undergone by the men operating them.[2] This proposal, although at the time turned down by the employers, was important in principle, for it meant that the union, then still a craft union, renounced the claim to apprenticeship being the exclusive entrance to skilled engineering occupations. Employers on their part drew on the experience of war-time dilution by upgrading semi-skilled operatives to do 'skilled men's work' and paying them at skilled rates,[3] without however consulting the trade union.

Dilution schemes in the second World War were similar to those developed in the first. Yet the aftermath was different: in 1919, the pre-war practices were quickly and smoothly

---

[1] 'No skilled man should be employed on work which can be done by semi-skilled or unskilled male or female labour'. Report re Dilution of Skilled Labour, Central Munitions Labour Supply Committee, Circular L5. Quoted by G. D. H. Cole, *Trade Unionism and Munitions*, p.93 (1923).

[2] Jefferys, *op. cit.*, p.246.

[3] ibid, p.206.

restored;[1] after 1945, dilution has not been discontinued in the engineering industry, but the trade unions exercise a large measure of control. This development must be considered in connection with the transformation of the A.E.U. into a multi-grade union. In 1926 it formed two new sections for non-skilled workers (several earlier attempts had been abortive). Since then, the union represents both the rival classes, craftsmen and unapprenticed workers, although many of the latter continue to join one of the General Unions. At present, the situation is governed by the Codified Agreement on Temporary Relaxation of Existing Customs (Dilution) which the A.E.U. and the Federation of Engineering Employers concluded in 1954. This document is the latest effort to come to terms in a protracted battle. It is interesting both by what it lays down and by what it leaves to 'reservations to be mutually agreed.' 'Where it can be shown that skilled men are not available, an alternative class of worker may be employed' instead of craftsmen. 'In the case of machining, the employer shall be allowed to put men of a semi-skilled character on the machines previously operated by skilled men . . .'

Dilution under the agreement takes place on a large scale, we were told by both sides of the engineering industry; figures on the number of dilutees are not available.

The procedure laid down (in Clause 6 of the Agreement) is that an employer has to apply for the Union's consent to a 'change of practice', viz. of putting unapprenticed workers on jobs previously done by skilled men; if the shop stewards approve, the dilution is endorsed by the A.E.U.'s and the employers' representatives on the Local Joint Relaxation Committee; the respective job and the names of individual dilutees are registered on standard forms, and 'when skilled labour becomes available restoration to the pre-Agreement practice shall be made.' This procedure gives the trade union a handle for regulating the supply of labour for occupations which have by custom been the prerogative of apprenticed men.

However, the union's control of dilution goes beyond that

[1] Industry reverted to traditional production methods: Cole, . . . *Munitions*, p.213ff, on the slowness of adapting war-time mass-production methods to peacetime uses.

provided for in the Agreement. A dilutee of five years' standing can be transferred by the A.E.U.'s local branch (with the approval of the Executive Council) into Section 1 of the union and thereby becomes subject to the trade union rules and regulations which restrict the employment of craftsmen. The employer has no say in this recognition of dilutees as skilled workers.

While in the A.E.U.'s agreement with the employers the matter is not mentioned, an almost identical situation is made explicit in an agreement covering a particular engineering trade, viz. on the Upgrading of Foundry Personnel :

'The Trade Unions among themselves have accepted the principle that a man on being upgraded should become associated with the Trade Union appropriate to the class of work to which he is upgraded. In accordance with the Procedure Agreements existing and the traditional position between the parties *this is a matter domestic to the man and the Unions, concerning which the Employers have no standing.* Subject to this undertaking the Employers would not regard an arrangement, whereby a man upgraded to a skilled job changed his membership to a skilled Trade Union, as being inappropriate.'[1]

The procedure of creating craftsmen without apprenticeship resembles closely that of conferring craftsman's status on apprentices, viz. in the division of parts played by employer and trade union. The apprentice has his indentures endorsed by his employer, but his skilled ticket is issued by the trade union; correspondingly, the dilutee is put to skilled work by the employer, but it is the trade union which transfers him into its skilled section.

The admission of dilutees to skilled status has several important aspects. One is that it deals a blow to the concept of apprentice-trained craftsmanship. Further, when the upgrading of unapprenticed workers cannot be prevented, it is obviously in the interest of the craftsmen, lest they be undercut and ousted by dilutees, that these should not only be paid 'the rate for the job,' but also be subject to demarcation and to the regulation forbidding their employment at less than skilled rates. By imposing these stipulations, the craft section of the A.E.U. also retains to some degree its exclusive character.

[1] Collective Agreement, 1946, Clause 5. Our italics.

In the interest of its semi-skilled members, on the other hand, the union must aim at obtaining skilled rates for the greatest possible number. The opening of skilled jobs to dilutees bestows on the latter the privileges of craftsmen without the sacrifices involved in serving an apprenticeship.

In these circumstances the A.E.U.'s policy of restricting the supply of skilled labour is involved: on the one hand, the policy aims at safeguarding the prerogative of its skilled members; on the other hand, apprenticeship-trained men are used as pace-makers for the wage claims of workers not so trained.[1] The trade unions' dilution policy benefits craftsmen at one time and upgraded operatives at another time. In conditions of full employment, the dilutees are the beneficiaries, by sharing the craftsmen's privileges; when trade is slack, the craftsmen are the beneficiaries because dilution has a cushioning effect on the security of their employment: by ensuring that in a recession dilutees have to make room for apprenticed men, craft unions and craft sections retain a measure of control over the supply of labour to their trades.

We have tried to ascertain at what points and by what methods trade unions' restrictive practices aimed at regulating entry are based on apprenticeship. Two important questions arise in this context: what has been the success of trade-union policy of regulating entry? and in what respects do trade unions' vested interests conflict with the National interest?

THE MEASURE OF SUCCESS IN REGULATING ENTRY

In *Engineering*, most trade unions have at first view well-nigh lost control of the supply of labour: the great majority of jobs are no longer craftsmen's work but that of semi-skilled operatives; and to jobs still recognised as skilled men's work, operatives are upgraded in great numbers. But the procedure of upgrading is governed by the Agreement on the Relaxation of Existing Customs (Dilution). Under this agreement, as has been shown, the Unions exercise considerable influence over

---

[1] In the case of dilutees, it may be said, the narrowing of wage differentials is complete : the differential is zero ! See p.172 on the narrowing of differentials.

dilution,[1] in two ways. First, by the stipulation that upgrading is only temporary: 'when skilled labour becomes available', i.e. in a recession, dilutees have to step down; dilution thus protects craftsmen against redundancy, although by regulation of exit rather than of entry. Second, trade unions restrict the supply of labour for the skilled occupations by making dilutees sooner or later[2] subject to demarcation rules and similar other regulations. Thus, while the monopoly of apprentice-trained craftsmen has been allowed to weaken, the measures restricting the supply of labour which used to be the exclusive characteristic of apprenticed men, are now extended to a much larger section of the labour market.

A way of infiltration into skilled occupations over which the trade unions have no direct control is employment in non-union shops. Such firms remain outside employers' federations and are thus not parties to collective agreements. This does not mean that all non-federated firms disregard the agreements and existing customs concerning demarcation and dilution; but a number of firms, mainly small ones, do so.[3] Our informants have understandably been reluctant to make definite statements on this matter, and no figures are available which would make possible an estimate of the number of such firms. But it seems safe to conclude that this kind of infiltration into skilled trades is slight in the engineering industry compared with the building industry, where small non-federated firms abound.

Printing

In Printing, the craft unions have been uncommonly successful in controlling entry into their trades. Demarcation is laid down in the industry's National Scheme by the specification of separate apprenticeable trades. Dilution is, on the whole, effectively precluded by trade practice; war-time agreements in

---

[1] It is interesting that as early as 1915 the Clyde workers favoured dilution as 'a step in the direct line of industrial evolution', but demanded that it 'must be carried out under the control of the workers'; otherwise 'they would fight the scheme to the death'. *The Worker*, 15th January, 1916, and *Forward*, 1st January, 1916 respectively, quoted by J. B. Jefferys, *op. cit.*, p.178.

[2] In the A.E.U., after five years; in the Foundry Unions, on upgrading.

[3] The purpose of cutting wage rates, by contrast, is not now an important motive for firms' remaining outside employers' associations—see H. A. Clegg, 'Employers', in Flanders & Clegg, *op. cit.*, p.246/7.

which the trade unions accepted dilution have been discontinued. All the same, the introduction of new processes and new machines has caused, and continues to cause, protracted demarcation troubles between craft unions.[1] In some cases, too, dilution has had to be conceded, e.g. for rotary machine minding ('equal rights' clause in an agreement of 1918 between the T.A. and the N.A.T.S.O.P.A., a Union representing non-skilled printing workers), and more recently for the working of the photo-composing machine: every second vacancy in this job is to be filled by an experienced semi-skilled operator. An interesting feature is that the job in question has not been opened entirely to non-craftsmen all at once: the 50/50 agreement points the way in which older craftsmen's status can be protected even though their trade, having become de-skilled, is removed from the list of apprenticeable trades. A relaxation of a novel kind is contained in the 1956 agreement: the Amalgamated Society of Lithographic Printers agreed to the admission of twenty-five semi-skilled operatives per annum, after three years' training, to full craft status, and the acceptance of persons over eighteen years of age in these cases and in the case of annually twenty apprentices for five years.[2] These measures had been among the recommendations of a Productivity Team Report in 1951.[3]

The very clauses conceding relaxations bring out in full relief the tight control which the printers' unions exercise over the entry into their trades; the supply of labour is severely restricted, and there is little opportunity for entry into the printing trades by 'foreigners'. Yet the stringent demarcation and anti-dilutionism of the printers' unions have not been able entirely to prevent circumvention of the restrictive stipulations.

The operation of new machines and new processes within the printing industry has been brought under the control of the printers' unions, but these have no influence, or not much influence, over relevant developments outside the industry: the main challenge to the monopolistic position of apprenticed

---

[1] See Musson, op. cit., p.392.

[2] A 'block' of 100 apprentices above those permitted by the ratios was allowed to be taken into the industry, spread over five years.

[3] Anglo-American Council on Productivity, *Lithographic Printing*, p. 19.

printers, as well as competition to the printing industry, comes from the introduction and increasing use of office machines. Office machines are not difficult to work, and their product is not much different from that of printing machines proper. There are machines which are on the borderline between printing and office machines and which are used both in printing houses by professional printers and in offices by clerical staff, amateur printers as it were. On at least one firm making such an offset printing machine, the printing unions forced the undertaking to sell it only to printing houses, threatening that otherwise union members would not man this machine at the printers'. Another policy said to have been tried by the printing unions in order to eliminate the competition of office machines has so far been unsuccessful, viz. the effort to coerce the clerical staff who work office machines to become members of a printing union.

Building

In Building, as has been shown previously, large sections of the industry are outside the influence of the trade unions, viz. the workers employed by the host of non-federated small builders and those working in labour-only sub-contracting. Entry into the building trades by way of these two types of organisation being beyond the trade unions' control, the Unions' hostility against them is not surprising.[1]

In that area of the industry where collective bargaining prevails, demarcation between crafts is laid down, just as it is in Printing, by the specification of trades in which separate apprenticeships are available; the various crafts are organised in separate unions. Vertical demarcation is weak; there are no dilution agreements, but the craft unions themselves practise de-facto dilution by admitting members who have not served a proper apprenticeship, in order to counteract the employment of less-skilled men as cheap labour. If a man, having worked for two years as a bricklayer or plasterer (or in another building trade; the by-passing of apprenticeship in this way is

---

[1] It seems worth noting that 'many of the ablest of craftsmen gravitate towards labour-only'. (Article in *The Builder*, 14th October, 1955, reproduced in *The Operative Builder*, Vol. 9, No. 1, p.12).

least easy in plumbing, we were told) is sponsored by two members of a craft union, he is given the skilled ticket. Employers play no part in this creation of craftsmen without apprenticeship and are found to complain that they have to pay the skilled rate to men who are not, in fact, skilled. But, as was pointed out twenty years ago, 'responsibility for the existence of workmen who are entitled to, but do not deserve, a skilled wage must be divided between the unions and the employers . . . [by whom] the agreed standard wage rates are not uniformly observed.'[1]

On the face of it, the situation in Building closely resembles that under the dilution arrangements in Engineering. In fact, the circumstances are very dissimilar. Whereas in Engineering (and to some extent also in Printing) the craft unions have agreed to the employment of unapprenticed workers in a number of jobs which used to be claimed as 'skilled men's work', the building craft unions have not. Their practice of issuing the skilled ticket to non-apprenticed workers is a measure of despair: in principle, they are violently hostile to dilution.[2] What is remarkable is that the building unions have been backed in this attitude by employers' federations, by advisers from outside the industry and by the Government. Early in 1943, a 'Report on Training for the Building Industry' was published by the Education Committee of the Central Council for Works and Buildings. The Committee's opinion was later summarized thus: 'the first objective was to secure that no person should enter the Industry as a skilled worker unless he had been properly trained ('The backdoor to the Industry must be closed')'.[3] This uncompromising stand for the traditional sharp differentiation between skilled and non-skilled workers led to the formulation of an unrealistic apprenticeship scheme. The result is that the National Apprenticeship Scheme for the Building Industry is flouted by large numbers of non-federated small builders who employ

---

[1] *Are Trade Unions Obstructive?* p. 37.

[2] See 'Pages from Our History: Dilution,' by H. H., in *The Operative Builder*, Vol. 9, Nos. 1-3 (1956).—An exception to the hostility to dilution occurred after the last war: the building unions agreed to the acceptance of ex-servicemen as adult trainees, to the extent of 200,000 spread over five years (ibid., No. 3, p.186).

[3] B.A.T.C., *Third Report*, para, 105.

unapprenticed men in craftsmen's jobs, in defiance of both demarcation and non-dilution.

CONFLICT BETWEEN TRADE UNIONS' VESTED INTERESTS IN APPRENTICESHIP AND THE NATIONAL INTEREST

In one way or another, the national interest (and in the 'nation' we include the whole body of the manual workers) is impaired by all three sets of trade-union provisions for regulating entry into the skilled occupations—limitation of apprentices; long-term service and rigid age limits; and closing the trade to outsiders.

As a factor in the contriving of artificial scarcity, apprenticeship plays a two-fold part: one direct and one indirect. Direct restriction is brought about through limitation of apprentices; indirectly, apprenticeship acts as a restrictive device, because it helps to buttress the system of restrictive practices associated with the strict demarcation of jobs.

Direct limitation of the number of apprentices prevails in the printing trades. The scarcity of printers contrived by very rigid apprentice ratios (reinforced by strict demarcation) does benefit the special groups of workers who practice these restrictions; but this is at the expense of the rest of the community, who receive unnecessarily slow and dear services from the printing industry. It must be mainly ascribed to this situation that labour and capital have been diverted to the manufacture of office machines, causing productive resources to be maldistributed among their possible uses. Nor is this the only consequent loss to the country's economy: because of the high cost of printing here, British publishers have English books for the home market printed in Holland and other Continental countries—an inexpedient import which has adverse effects on the country's balance of payments.

To the workers who are unable to obtain a foothold in the protected occupations, the inequity is less than it was formerly. Full employment; the multiplication of well-paid jobs outside the conventional hierarchies; technical changes in the old skilled trades, with the consequent growth in the number of semi-skilled workers and of dilutees: all these have tended to reduce the effects of a limitation of apprentices. In fact, except in the printing and a few other trades with strict apprentice ratios, limitation of the number of apprentices is not now an important feature of trade unions' apprenticeship policy.

The indirectly restrictive effects of apprenticeship are far more important nowadays. In all the industries investigated, demarcation rules are laid down. Demarcation practices have the result that more men are engaged upon a job than would be necessary with a rational division of labour; they also add to the time, and therefore to the cost, of doing the work.[1] In other words, demarcation reduces productivity, and the community is the poorer for it.

It is therefore to be regretted that in Engineering the application of demarcation has been greatly extended: it used to be practised only by apprenticed craftsmen, not by less-skilled workers; now, however, dilutees become subject to the demarcation rules and similar practices when they are transferred to the A.E.U.'s craft section. This means increased obstacles to the efficient deployment of a firm's labour and thus a heavier drag on productivity.

The trade unions' insistence on a five-year term and on narrowly fixed age limits for beginning and completion of apprenticeship is harmful to the national interest in another way: the rigidity of the apprenticeship regulations impedes the occupational mobility of labour. Adaptability to economic and technical change is vital to any dynamic economic system and particularly so to one which is on the threshold of automation. Unemployment can be kept at bay only if it is possible for adult workers to train or retrain when their previous jobs become redundant through technical development.

Sectional interests in apprenticeship are at variance with the general interest also in the matter of adjusting the coverage of the apprenticeship system to the altered demand for skill. Trades which have been de-skilled are still claimed to be apprenticeable trades, and ex-apprentices in such trades are

---

[1] It is only fair to the institution of apprenticeship to observe that demarcation can exist without apprenticeship and that apprenticeship does not necessarily entail demarcation.

admitted to craftsman's status and privileges. This unrealistic conservatism has harmful repercussions in many directions. One of them is the tortuous procedure of dilution by which great numbers of unapprenticed workers enter 'skilled' occupations. Dilution, however, is accompanied by socially undesirable conditions. These circumstances make for trouble and friction in industrial relations.

Another damaging effect is the discouragement of real skill. One-job craftsmen are bracketed with highly skilled men (precision workers and all-round craftsmen) as entitled to differential wage rates. In the case of the highly skilled men, wage differentials are economically justified; in the case of the others, they are not. The narrowing of differentials which has been such a prominent feature of the post-war time does no injustice to one-skill men, but it victimizes craftsmen of superior skill. The line dividing craftsmen from less-skilled workers ought to be raised above its conventional level so that differential rates become the due only of workers of high skill or superior responsibility.

The narrowing of wage differentials does not belong in the present argument, although both issues are connected with the de-skilling of crafts. Mr. H. A. Turner[1] rejects the effect of technical development (viz. de-skilling) as an explanation of the decline in skill differentials; his thesis is that the narrowing of differentials is due to the development of trade unionism itself, one of the main features being the emergence of great unions which cater for many different grades and which compete for members with general unions (p.275). But this argument does not dispose of de-skilling as a reason for the narrowing of differentials, for the transformation of such craft unions as the A.E.U. into multi-grade unions has been closely bound up with the de-skilling of traditional trades. If there had not been a change in the real system of relative scarcities underlying the labour-market situation, the shift in relative wages would soon have corrected itself.

Mr. Turner makes however the interesting point that in the engineers' wage claims of 1949-50, the former craft unions

[1] 'Trade Unions, Differentials and the Levelling of Wages' in *Manchester School*, September, 1952, pp.227-282).

(A.E.U. and E.T.U.) advocated a flat increase, involving a narrowing of differentials, whereas the two general unions made 'a proposal that . . . was commonly taken to imply a reconstruction of differentials in which the semi-skilled and *very skilled* would receive particular attention' (p.249, footnote). Our italics.

In recent decades circumstances have changed so greatly that the use to which the apprenticeship system is put by trade unionism is no longer quite the traditional one. Protection of the craftsmen's privileged position has ceased to be the single object: large numbers of less-skilled workers participate (at least temporarily) in the apprenticed men's privileges and in their restrictive practices. Moreover, the restrictions which benefit the protected groups are now less prejudicial to the rest of the workers, mainly because of the narrowing of wage differentials and because of increasing opportunities in other occupations.

In spite of all this, however, apprenticeship is still instrumental in effecting a deleterious Institutional Restriction[1] of the supply of labour. Today, the chief harm caused by demarcation and other restrictive practices is inflicted, not upon less-favoured workers qua workers, nor, in the short run, upon the incomes from the other factors of production, but upon the country's productivity and therefore upon the whole people as consumers.

---

[1] This concept was developed by Professor H. D. Dickinson in *Institutional Revenue: A Study of the Influence of Social Institutions on the Distribution of Wealth* (1932); for Institutional Restriction and labour, in particular, see pp.156-161, also pp.165-167.

X

APPRENTICESHIP IN A RURAL AREA

A COMPARISON WITH CONDITIONS IN BRISTOL

THE area chosen as the principal basis of the rural part of this enquiry is the Eastern Mendips in North Somerset; but, as pointed out in the Introduction, relevant information from other rural areas has been freely used. Consequently, by no means all statements in this chapter refer to the particular area in Somerset.

The area is hilly; it is poor farming land, thinly populated and interspersed with country towns which are industrialised to varying degrees. These towns range in size from 5,000 to 12,000 inhabitants. While not very far apart from each other in terms of mileage, they are only moderately well interconnected by public transport services. On the whole, the towns constitute separate labour markets; each of these is therefore small and limited in variety; nor are large labour markets (Bristol and Bath) within easy daily reach. There is no technical college either in the area or easily accessible.

This type of rural area was selected in order to show apprenticeship conditions which are markedly different from those in a city: neither a purely agricultural area nor a more fully industrialised rural area such as the Stroud Valleys, where varified industrial plants are fairly closely grouped, would have served that purpose.

The institution of apprenticeship plays a comparatively small part in the social and economic life of rural areas. This is due to several factors: entry into agricultural occupations has never been subject to apprenticeship;[1] most rural crafts have declined; industrial craftsmanship is essentially an urban development and not deeply rooted in rural society; and craft unions, the main champions of apprenticeship, are not so influential outside fully industrialised areas.

There is yet another factor which is less obvious. Today, a considerable proportion of the industrial establishments in rural and semi-rural areas are but rump firms: their managerial functions are restricted in range and/or in vigour. This state of affairs has been brought about by two developments: first, most new factories established under the decentralisation-of-industry policy are branches of firms whose main seat is in London or another big centre; second, many an old local firm has lost its independence by becoming the subsidiary of a non-local company or by joining a group of firms. *Ceteris paribus* both these types of factory in rural areas offer less good training facilities (as well as less interesting work and less good chances of promotion) than a fully-fledged firm with its headquarters and all departments in one place.

Attenuation of this kind varies in degree; but even in a large and lively works the training of apprentice draughtsmen is liable to be adversely affected by an arrangement under which the primary designs are made at the firm's headquarters in London, while the drawing office attached to the works is left with the development of more detailed designs and the preparation of the detail drawings for use on the shopfloor.

DEMAND FOR AND SUPPLY OF APPRENTICES

The rural area displays considerable local variations in the demand for and supply of apprentices. In a small labour market, even one firm of medium size may make a great difference in the situation. Where a modern factory with openings for apprentices has been set up, the new opportunities for local boys will raise the number of would-be apprentices. In a quiescent country town, on the other hand, whose established firms let things take their course and which has not

---

[1] Recent efforts to develop apprenticeship in agriculture have not been very successful.

attracted new industry, the demand for apprentices is modest both in quantity and in quality; nor does there appear to exist a substantial unsatisfied desire for apprenticeship openings.

No statistical data are available on the boys who move from the rural area to become apprentices in larger labour markets; but it seems safe to say that the number is small. It includes some grammar-school pupils who leave home to enter higher-grade apprenticeships and a few cases of away-from-home apprenticeship sponsored by the Special Aptitudes Scheme. This Scheme (since 1956 called Training Allowances Scheme) was introduced in 1947 'to enable suitable boys and girls to take a course of training for a skilled occupation away from home where no suitable facilities are available within daily travelling distance of their homes'.[1] The Y.E.S. decides on the eligibility of applicants for the grants under the Scheme and finds the apprenticeship openings. In practice, the Scheme has been used mainly to assist boys and girls from remote rural areas where not only training facilities but employment opportunities altogether are poor.

The fact that there has been not more than a trickle of boys from the rural area into apprenticeships elsewhere is by no means just a reflection of immobility on the part of young persons in villages and small towns: it reflects also the shortage of apprenticeship openings in the country as a whole. The special impact on rural areas of the over-all scarcity of openings is held up to view by a modification of the Special Aptitudes Scheme. In 1954 the C.Y.E.E.

'made it a condition of transfer to any particular area that the young person should not deprive a local boy or girl of an opportunity to take up training. This restriction has been placed on the scheme because it has in practice proved too difficult to determine satisfactorily which of any two young persons in different areas is the better suited for training in any particular post. It is also not considered justifiable to give assistance from public funds for the transfer of young persons where this would mean that suitable local candidates would remain unemployed, or would be deprived of apprenticeships for which they were considered suitable.'[2]

---

[1] Recommendation of the Ince Committee: Report, para. 134.
[2] *The Work of the Y.E.S.* 1953-1956, p.12.

Under the assisted Scheme, therefore, would-be apprentices from rural areas find themselves, through official regulation, at the tail-end of the queue;[1] it stands to reason that the same situation prevails unofficially, in the ordinary search for openings, outside the Scheme. By and large, rural aspirants to the scarce apprenticeship openings, most of which are offered in big labour markets, have less chance of acceptance than local boys. Rural boys are, however, not so handicapped in the competition for apprenticeship openings where the recruitment depends on elaborate selection rather than on personal contacts. Thus the B.A.C. has a fair number of apprentices from rural areas, and so have other firms of the Scientific Apprentice Management type, especially in the higher-grade apprenticeships.

To return to the apprenticeship market in the rural area itself, employers there, like those in more fully industrialised areas, complain about the quality of recruits for apprenticeship. Complaints about the low educational standard of candidates appear to be more justified in some parts of rural areas than they are in Bristol. One ancient town which we visited was still without a secondary modern school and made do with an old-type all-age school. In another town, the two secondary modern schools, with 700 and 500 children respectively, were crowded.

In a rural area, a new modern firm with high entry standards may not find a ready pool of the right calibre of recruits for apprenticeship. The selection officer of such a works told us that with nearly three times as many applications as apprenticeship openings he had not enough choice.[2] A small, old-established heavy-engineering firm in the same town resigns

---

[1] The situation has been somewhat redressed through a further modification of the conditions of the Training Allowance Scheme (*Ministry of Labour Gazette*, March, 1958, p.99). But the Y.E.S. is now responsible for ensuring that the claims of local candidates for apprenticeship openings are not overlooked. Moreover, beneficiaries under the Scheme are not always rural boys: at least one Bristol youth is at present assisted to serve an Engineering apprenticeship in a rural area.

[2] By comparison, an average of three to four applications per available apprentice place was reported with great satisfaction in the B.A.C.'s house magazine *The 'Bristol' Quarterly* in 1954 (Vol. 1, No. 5, p.123). Other employers will not say more than that they have a waiting list of aspirants to apprenticeship.

itself to accepting less suitable apprentices than formerly, since E.M.I. now recruits the best ones.

Elsewhere, a printing firm is rather dissatisfied with the educational level of modern-school pupils (very few of the firm's printing apprentices are grammar-school boys). On the other hand, two engineering firms in the town, both engaged in heavy non-precision work, are satisfied that the modern-school education of their apprentices suffices for the kinds of job they are expected to do.

In the south-western part of the rural area, builders have difficulties in recruiting sufficient numbers of apprentices even in carpentry, the best-liked building trade. This is due to the strong competition for young workers by the large and growing shoe-manufacturing firm of Clark's at Street. Although there exists no apprenticeship proper in Boot and Shoe Manufacture, this firm competes for school-leavers of apprentice calibre. For it has a training scheme by which selected young workers as well as new entrants recruited from grammar schools and secondary technical schools can receive, in the Factory Training School, technical education leading to the Intermediate and Final C. & G. examinations; it also offers higher careers in its shoe-research and shoe-design departments.

Firms are liable to recruit apprentices from a wide area, covering the surrounding countryside over a radius of many miles—especially firms which demand good educational qualifications and offer attractive apprenticeships. The main example in the area under review is the new establishment of E.M.I. at Wells, a firm in a new industry (electronic equipment) which appeals to the imagination of boys; the firm recruits nearly half of its apprentices from grammar schools and one-quarter from secondary technical schools; some of these are in towns at considerable distances from Wells. The Westinghouse Co. at Chippenham also recruits a large proportion of its higher-trade apprentices from towns outside the Chippenham area. While non-local recruiting is most frequent for higher-grade apprenticeships in Engineering, in other industries, too, some apprenticeships are taken up by boys from far afield. In one town an eight-mile radius was stated as the catchment area for building-trade apprentices; two printing apprentices were recruited from places 14 to 20 miles away.

TRAINING

Apprentice training in the rural area shows in several respects the influence of conditions which are inherent in, or connected with, the smallness of the labour markets. An industrial plant will often be the only one of a given industry or section of industry in the area. This reduces labour turnover: the firm finds it much more difficult than works located in a large labour market to recruit craftsmen or technicians trained by other firms, and workers have little choice of jobs within easy reach. Except in Printing, trade-union influence is not so strong and there is less insistence on demarcation and on the distinction between craftsmen and non-apprenticed workers.

To these conditions employers of apprentices respond in various ways. Nearly all kinds of firms in rural areas freely employ non-skilled labour in some jobs which are in most Bristol firms reserved to craftsmen (or conditionally open to dilutees).

In Engineering, the less enterprising employers rely on the lack of alternative local openings and on the immobility of the workers: in some firms the number of apprentices is very small in proportion to the number of craftsmen, and jobs are filled with semi-skilled men; in other firms the apprentice ratio is higher but the standard of training is low.

Active and alert employers, by contrast, are not only aware of the necessity to train their own workers, but also intent on producing versatile craftsmen who can be put to work in any of the firm's departments. Their apprentices will therefore receive an all-round training (in a large engineering works with several divisions apprentices were indeed heard to complain about overmuch moving on). Much care is bestowed by firms of this type on the development of higher-grade apprenticeships for the training of technicians and technologists. At the same time, such a firm may discard apprenticeship for most machining jobs and train non-apprenticed boys for these. The de-skilling of machining has gone farther than that of fitting; machining is unpopular as a skilled trade—it is monotonous and carries lower pay than fitting. There are one or two skilled machining jobs, chiefly turning, but keen turners are said to aspire to a technician's standing, perhaps as a planning engineer.

An unorthodox method of training for engineering trades was adopted in a place which offered no pool of labour with industrial experience. A firm (owners of a local garage), on setting up the first manufacturing plant in a residential and holiday town, developed a trainee scheme under which men up to about 30 years are 'taken from the street' and put in the firm's training shop for 6 weeks before going on production; after five years they can be upgraded to skilled workers of the one-skill type. The scheme is, the director claims, a blessing for ex-servicemen who missed the bus of apprenticeship.

Training for the building trades in rural areas is conditioned by the fact that building is a service industry indigenous to the countryside. At least one jobbing builder can be found in every sizable village and in many a smaller one. Building firms are small, most of them very small; their business consists pre-dominantly of maintenance and repair work; trade-union influence is weak; and facilities for appropriate technical education are not within easy reach.

These circumstances do not favour the strict compliance with the stipulations of the National Apprenticeship Scheme of the Building Industry. The particular difficulties of securing the apprentices' technical education in rural areas will be dealt with in the next section. As regards training on the job, demarcation between the several building trades is not so rigid in the countryside, and an apprentice who is indentured as a bricklayer will not be strictly kept to his own trade but will become acquainted also with other building trades. He will get less practice in new building work than the town apprentice employed by a large contractor; but country firms claim that their apprentices get more varied experience on different sites and on intricate repair jobs.

Plastering is done by general building firms in one part of the area under review, and their apprentices include a few plasterers. In the rest of the area, builders subcontract this work to a plastering contractor or to 'a plasterer and his mate.'

In these cases, plasterer craftsmen and apprentices are kept to their own trade because their employers specialise in this type of work.

The foregoing observations refer to building firms whose apprentices are indentured under the National Apprenticeship Scheme of the industry; by rural standards, these are large building firms, employing craftsmen of several trades and also labourers. But many very small builders, especially in villages, have no use for specialisation of trades or for differentiation between craftsmen and less-skilled workers: each of their men is more or less competent in various building trades, and this composite kind of skill is passed on to the boys employed by such builders. In small building firms training shades off imperceptively into producing the handy-man type of craftsman.[1]

Training for the printing trades in the rural areas is, just as it is in cities, under the sway of the trade unions. Jobs in the printing trades are reserved to apprenticed journeymen and the system of apprentice ratios is applied unremittingly. This allows comparatively ample numbers of apprentices to be employed by the small printing firms engaged in local business, but limits severely the number of apprentices who may be trained by a large printing house; at the time of our visit to a particular firm, its apprentice entitlement was less than half the number needed to replace the journeymen who were nearing retiring age.

This printing house is one of the last, if not the last, in this country in which some women operate composing machines. Their employment as keyboard operator or casting-machine operator dates back to well before the last war, when the firm's manpower policy was not yet under the control of the Typographical Association. When the firm became a 'recognised house'—recognised, that is to say, by the T.A., which fights the admission of female compositors[2]—the individual women and girls were allowed to keep their jobs, but no other females were to be put in their places. The number of these old female

---

[1] See chapters 4 and 9 for the discussion, from various angles, of the by-passing of formal building apprenticeship.

[2] See A. E. Musson, *op. cit.*, p.390; also *Women in the Printing Trades*, Editor J. Ramsay Macdonald, Preface by F. Y. Edgeworth, *passim* (1904).

compositors is now dwindling through retirement; this adds to the firm's desperate shortage of young printers, especially since the women have not been reckoned as journeymen in the calculation of the firm's apprentice entitlement.

TECHNICAL EDUCATION

The absence of a local or other easily accessible college imposes a handicap on apprentice training in the rural area. That this fact is liable to retard local industrial development was demonstrated after the end of the war when an instrument-making firm which had been evacuated to the area was invited to remain there for good: the firm refused because of the lack of training facilities for its skilled workers and technicians. By now, some progress has been made in the provision of local facilities for technical education. In the largest town of the area (which is however not centrally located) certain C. & G. part-time day courses in engineering and building subjects are now held, viz. in machine shop engineering and in building construction. Apprentices in other trades are still not provided for locally; and it may be argued that foundry apprentices are not necessarily 'blockheads' (as one employer called them, adding that they would become very good moulders nevertheless), if they refuse to attend a technical course which is not designed for foundry workers.

The lack of local facilities for technical education drove an instrument-making firm from the rural areas. Since then another works with a similar kind of product, but larger and Government-backed, has been established in the same town. This firm's apprentices who come to work from all directions were sent to the technical colleges nearest to their homes; the result was that the firm had to deal with four different colleges, a state of affairs which is not conducive to the desirable close contact between employer and technical college. In 1956 the firm itself, having procured the backing of the L.E.A., started a course locally. A science graduate with technical-teaching experience in the Forces was engaged as training officer and for holding an S.1 course (the first-year of the O.N.C. course) one day a week. Since the scheme is subsidised by the L.E.A., apprentices of other firms have the right to attend this course. At the time of our interview, however, only one of the 14 students was apprenticed to another firm. Perhaps more outsiders will join as the existence of the course becomes more widely known. But one factor adverse to such development will remain, viz. that the course is focused on the particular requirements of the firm conducting the course, which are not likely to be shared by other engineering firms in the vicinity.

The attendance of trowel-trade apprentices at the general-building course has been so little successful that it is being contemplated to send bricklayer and plasterer apprentices out of the county to a college which caters for their own trades. Throughout the area, many small building employers use the fact that appropriate courses are not easily accessible to ignore their obligation (under the National Apprenticeship Scheme) to release apprentices during working hours, and many apprentices use it to evade their obligation to attend evening classes. A scheme of the Building Department of the College of Technology, Bristol, for block-release courses for apprentice plasterers from rural areas met with very poor response and was dropped.[1]

A similar attitude to technical education prevails among not-so-large printing firms in the rural area (in the printing industry, however, attendance at courses is not a condition of apprenticeship). 'We can teach our boys equally well here' was the view of one manager; the same firm, however, and smaller ones as well, has found it worth while to send apprentices to Bristol for several weeks' full-time instruction at the monotype school: firms obviously realize that the elements of this highly mechanical way of printing cannot be equally well taught in the workshop.

The number of printing apprentices being kept small by the ratio agreements, printing courses are held at few technical colleges only, and Bristol is the teaching centre for a wide area, in some subjects for the whole S.W. Region. Printing apprentices in rural areas have therefore long journeys to and from their weekly day-cum-evening courses.

[1] The block-release scheme which was introduced for plasterer apprentices in the Bristol-Bath Area is discussed on p. 119.

APPRENTICESHIP IN A RURAL AREA

THE YOUTH EMPLOYMENT SERVICE

A comparison of the Y.E.S. in rural areas with that in Bristol reflects not only the difference between countryside and city but also the difference between the operation of the Service through the Ministry of Labour and through L.E.As respectively. The evidence on the Y.E.S. recently submitted to the Select Committee on Estimates (Sub-Committee E) is mainly concerned with the operation of the Service through L.E.As, but sheds some light also on the part of the Service that is administered directly by the M.o.L., mainly in rural and county areas.[1]

It is in the nature of the situation that the Y.E.S. is up against greater obstacles in rural areas than in town; in small labour markets it is more difficult to find the most suitable job for each school leaver, and in only partly industralised areas it is more difficult to make parents and teachers as well as the children aware of modern employment opportunities and modern educational requirements. However, the disadvantages under which the rural Y.E.O. has to work are enhanced by the organisation of Youth Employment work in areas where the Service is operated by the Ministry of Labour. The following discussion is meant to draw attention to the last-mentioned handicap; it is not offered as a balanced assessment of the work of the Y.E.S. in rural areas in general.

The Ministry of Labour Y.E.O. in a rural area is usually a junior official, liable to be transferred before very long to another area or to other duties: Y.E.S. is not a career of its own in the Ministry of Labour. In a thinly populated area, the Y.E.O.'s province is extensive; it may cover several Local-Office areas (the term Local Office denotes Employment

---

[1] Seventh Report from the Select Committee on Estimates, Session 1956-57: *The Youth Employment Service and Youth Service Grants.*

The rising costs of the heavily grant-aided youth employment work of the L.E.As were criticized by the Treasury witness (comparable figures on the cost of the Ministry of Labour's Y.E. work were not available). The Sub-Committee, however, was unable to find any evidence of extravagance in the administration of the Service and could therefore suggest no economies in the Estimates for the Y.E.S. consistent with the policy implied therein. (P.iv and Minutes of Evidence, *passim*).

Exchanges and smaller M.o.L. Offices). The range of his work, by contrast, is apt to be narrow: the two functions which are combined in the Bristol Youth Employment Office, vocational guidance and placing in employment, may be found to be separated in rural areas. In such cases the Y.E.O. performs only the former function: he visits the various secondary modern schools in his province to give talks and individual interviews to children in their last year at school. Placing, except in special cases, is not his function; it is done by the Managers of the Local Offices, who are on the spot and continuously in touch with local employers. The Y.E.O. is liable to lack the intimate knowledge of the local employment situation which comes from regular contacts; his advice to school leavers may therefore sometimes have to be given with inadequate local information.

The scope of the rural Y.E.O.'s work is further restricted by another division of functions. Whereas many L.E.As make one office responsible for the Y.E.S. for all young persons up to 18—the Bristol Youth Employment Office takes indeed particular pride in its careers-information work for older school leavers—the Ministry of Labour operates the Service in two parts: the service for school leavers up to 15+ is provided locally and performed by the Y.E.Os, but older school leavers, mainly grammar-school pupils, who wish to avail themselves of the Service are advised by Careers Advisory Officers who operate from the Ministry's regional headquarters. The service is operated in this way also in the fringe areas of Bristol, both urban and rural, and in Chippenham.

The arrangement has no doubt certain advantages: specially selected and trained staff can be used for advising boys who aim at higher careers, and it is more economical to centralize the services for the comparatively small number of such boys. But from the point of view of rural Y.E.Os the arrangement is disadvantageous. The fact that they are concerned only with modern schools lowers the regard in which they are held by schools, parents and employers; this as well as the limited experience allowed to many of them is liable to affect the usefulness of their work.

Conditions tend to be different in an area where the Youth

Employment work has been for a number of years in the charge of a higher-grade officer. He is a person of consequence in the district who is readily given information and whose advice carries greater weight; grammar schools are induced to use his services for pupils who leave school at 15 or 16, and he has occasion to disseminate careers information, even though it remains the responsibility of the Regional Careers Advisory Service to give individual advice on higher careers.

A comprehensive Y.E.S. was set up only after the last war; the Service is therefore faced with special staffing problems. The training of officers for the Service has been regarded as essentially a matter for long-term planning. The (Piercy) Committee on Recruitment and Training for the Youth Employment Service, reporting in 1951, emphasized the importance of comprehensive training. It recommended a full-time training course extending over one year; but for reasons of economy this has, with one exception, not yet been introduced.[1] The M.o.L. now runs a four-week course for newly appointed Y.E.Os; we would like to suggest the inclusion of industrial economics among the subjects of the course.

The work of the Y.E.S. in rural areas is beset with particular difficulties. The fact that many of them are inherent in the situation makes it all the more important that the rural Y.E.O.'s hand should be strengthened by the reduction of those difficulties which arise from the organisation of the Service.

---

[1] The exception is a course of an academic year at Lamorbey Park, organised by the Kent Education Authority in association with the University of Oxford Delegacy for Extra-Mural Studies; all students of this course go into the Y.E.S. operated by one or other L.E.A. (*The Work of the Y.E.S.* 1953-1956, pp.4/5).

XI

CONCLUSIONS

IT can be claimed that throughout its long history the apprenticeship system has adjusted itself in many ways to social, economic and technical changes. But certain features of critical importance have remained unaltered, namely the conditions deriving from the dual nature of apprenticeship and from its historical role as a social institution: apprenticeship is not just a form of training but is also used by both sides of industry in order to further their respective sectional interests. All the modifications made in adjustment to technical and other developments have been made in such a manner as to preserve the power of employers and trade unions to bend apprenticeship to their own ends.

This has been brought about by way of accommodation between the former antagonists: employers and trade unions have come to terms on the issue of apprenticeship; but the outcome is in various respects at variance with the national interest.

From the point of view of the national interest the criteria by which to judge the apprenticeship system can be grouped under these headings:

Supply of sufficient workers with requisite skills.

Efficiency and economy of training.

Effects on productivity.

The first two items concern apprenticeship as a system of training, the third as the basis of restrictive practices.

CONCLUSIONS

On the issue of the number of apprentices, the former controversy has almost ceased to exist, both sides of industry having changed their attitudes. Employers do not now desire to maximize the number of apprentices, for two reasons. First, the apprentices' labour is no longer so cheap: not only have their wages risen in proportion to adult wages, but firms have also to bear the cost of day release for their apprentices' technical education; second, many traditional crafts are de-skilled, and in the dilution agreements, the engineering unions have accepted the employment of semi-skilled operatives in 'skilled men's work', provided that no craftsmen are available.

In addition to this general weakening of firms' eagerness to take on apprentices, there are the effects of cyclical fluctuations and of Government decisions (e.g. that the aircraft industry must diminish its labour force) which lead to further reductions of the number of apprenticeship openings, at least temporarily. The employers' temporary cut in the intake of apprentices is turned into an irrecoverable loss of skilled manpower by the trade unions' insistence on rigid age limits for (and duration of) apprenticeship: unless the maximum age for beginning apprenticeship is raised beyond 16+, today's school leavers who are in excess of the reduced number of apprenticeship openings will be too old for apprenticeship when the number of openings comes to be raised. This waste of the country's manpower is all the more serious because it coincides with the 'bulge' in this particular age group.

In a few industries and trades (of which Printing is a notable example) craft unions still insist on apprentice ratios; but, on the whole, trade unions are no longer bent on limiting the number of apprentices; this old device for regulating entry into the skilled occupations has become ineffective, as masses of semi-skilled workers enter jobs which used to be reserved to craftsmen. On the other hand, it is not in the character either of craft unions or of the multi-grade unions into which the biggest craft unions in Engineering have been transformed to press for a large intake of apprentices. Thus, neither of the two sides of industry at present eagerly desires a high number of apprentices.

The Government's policy of using the apprenticeship system as virtually the only vehicle for promoting technical (and general) education of young workers is therefore faced with a slackening in the number of apprentices. More than that, the Government unwittingly defeats its object by confining its pressure for day release to apprentices. This (instead of making part-time education a statutory obligation for all young workers) puts an extra cost on the employment of apprentices and is thus a factor in lessening the number of apprenticeship openings offered by firms.

The employers' demand for skilled workers is in some respects larger, in other respects smaller than a sufficiency of workers with the requisite skills by the criterion of the national interest. Industry's demand for skilled workers is larger than that required in the national interest because, owing to trade-union pressure, posts in actually de-skilled trades have to be filled with apprenticed craftsmen; (and the intake of apprentices is unrelated to national requirements where firms employ apprentices in order to use them as cheap labour during their term of service, without wishing to keep them as craftsmen after the completion of their apprenticeship). On the other hand, industry's demand for skill is lower than that required in the national interest in that firms are liable to take a short view and, consulting only their own interest, train craft apprentices in a narrow range of specific skills, whereas the national interest calls for fuller training and for the extension of training to less-skilled workers; further, industry's intake of apprentices may be too small because firms reckon upon being able to employ tradesmen trained by other firms.

In view of this situation, it would appear that it is not in the best interests of the community that the number of apprentices should be left to be determined by industry itself.

REQUISITE SKILLS

Continual development in technique and workshop organisation has been drastically altering the requisite skills, both in kind and in incidence. Through increasing mechanisation and division of labour, many old trades have been reduced in degree and range of skill. The seat of the skill which goes into the making of a product has shifted from the shopfloor to the drawing office, the laboratory, the costing clerk's and the planning engineer's desks. (Since these semi-professional occupations have been drawn into the apprenticeship system, there are now apprenticeable occupations of disparate levels of requisite skill, ranging from one-job skill to technicians' and technologists' competence). However, the changes in kind and incidence of specific skills are only part of the whole development. While the manual dexterity and the experience required of many craftsmen have declined, there is for all workers in industry a growing need for higher standards of general education and of technical understanding.

The need for improved general and technical education derives in the first place from the employers' current demand, in the second place from long-term national requirements. In the prevailing dynamic conditions, flexibility of the economy is of vital importance for securing high productivity and maintaining high employment. What skills are requisite thus depends not only on present or easily foreseeable demand of industry, but also on uncertain future trends. The pace of technological development and of economic change is such that the existing number and occupational distribution of craftsmen is no sound indication of what number of apprentices ensures a sufficient supply of future craftsmen in a given trade. As automation spreads, in particular, many workers will have to expect that they cannot stay in one occupation during the whole of their working lives; in dynamic conditions, occupational and industrial mobility of labour is essential. This consideration greatly enhances the importance of technical and of general education; for it is education in all its forms (rather than the possession of specific skills) that facilitates mobility and adaptability.

For the same reason, it must be made easy for adults whose jobs become redundant to retrain for another occupation. The prevailing regulations, about which the trade unions have so far been unyielding, on age limits for apprenticeship and on its length cripple the adjustment to technical and economic change. The apprenticeship system will fail to supply workers of the requisite adaptability until it allows the retraining, of a duration dictated only by training needs, of workers over 21 years of age; if these have had a sound grounding in general and technical subjects as well as experience of working life, it is only specific skill which they have to learn anew. With modern training methods, the time required for such refresher courses, as it were, should be short; this is important, for it reduces the period of unemployment or of reduced earnings during re-training.

TRAINING PROBLEMS

The traditional and still popular ideal of all-round training in several closely related trades is not compatible with modern conditions. On all levels, today, the requisite skill consists of three parts:—specific practical skill, technical knowledge, and general education; the first has lost, the two others have gained in importance.

The monolithic character of apprentice training has been broken: to practical training has now been added technical education; since the latter is urged and provided (or subsidised) by the Government, the employer has ceased to bear the entire responsibility for apprentice training; and the single-type craft apprenticeship is being replaced by a grading of apprentice-ships.

The employer is still the arbiter of practical training: no minimum standards are laid down, let alone enforced; and no test of proficiency is required for the completion of apprentice-ship. There is consequently a great variety in the contents, the methods and the quality of training. By their training methods firms (and industries) fall into two groups: the traditional manner of training on the shopfloor or 'on the job' prevails in the printing and building industries and in most engineering firms; but in Engineering the modern method of separating training from production is gaining ground—in a number of firms, before going on to the shopfloor, apprentices receive basic training in a training workshop under special instructors.

CONCLUSIONS

Such training has many advantages over training on the shop-floor, which is liable to lack thoroughness, to be unsystematic and to impart indifferent skill. But the modern training method has, in practice though not inherently, one considerable disadvantage: it is often limited to a very narrow range of jobs.

This feature of modern training is, in Engineering, connected with the grading of apprenticeships. Although formal grading schemes have so far been introduced only by a minority of firms, informal grading prevails in a much wider field. Through grading, the organisation of apprenticeship is being reshaped in accordance with, and in turn increases, the vertical division of labour. The development is not only that a superstructure of higher-grade apprenticeships for technicians and technologists is being erected above craft apprenticeship. In addition, the old-style craft apprenticeship itself is being subdivided: de-skilled trades are demoted into a lower-grade craft apprenticeship. This lowest grade of apprenticeship trains for what is in fact (although it is never openly recognised as such) one-skill jobs.

Employers bear the cost of training and tend therefore to confine the training of apprentices to the skill required for the job which each is intended to do in the firm's service. Accordingly, the training of higher-grade apprentices, the future technicians and middle managers, is by and large satisfactory; but the future narrowly specialized craftsman gets narrow, specialized training and experience. (This contrasts with the not-so-thorough but wider training which is provided by training on the shop floor. In some firms, unfortunately, the worst features of both methods are combined: training is narrow as well as lacking in thoroughness). Apprentice grading is a rational procedure, but as arranged at present, it is not without serious drawbacks: the lower grades are being denuded of interest and responsibility, and their narrow or superficial training fails to make them adaptable.

Moreover, one advantage of systematic training by modern training methods adds by a side-wind to a deleterious effect of the de-skilling of trades: both make it possible for the skill required for a job to be imparted much more quickly than formerly. This shortening of the time of actual training however (usually to less, and mostly to very much less, than half the five years of apprenticeship) is a loss for 'character training': the habit of taking pains over a job was a by-product of the lengthy old-time training which needed much practice and experience; with the reduction of training time, good working habits are no longer produced as a by-product of acquiring specific skill.

The shift of emphasis from training in specific practical skill to technical and mathematical education constitutes a major adjustment of apprenticeship to modern requirements. The drive to make technical education an integral part of apprenticeship has been up against very great difficulties, and the success of the courses has so far been less than satisfactory. But it has to be realised that the shortcomings of technical education show up in the examinations, whereas the success of practical training is not put to the test: apprenticeship is completed after five years of service without proof of competence, by the mere lapse of time. The efforts which are now being made to improve technical education, appropriate to the various grades of apprenticeship, seem, on the whole, to promise well. Technical colleges have been extending their field of activity by including practical instruction in their courses, e.g. machine shop practice; this provides a useful complement to the know-how which apprentices are taught, or have to pick up, in a busy workshop. So far, however, general education figures vary little, if at all, in day-release courses.

Some enlightened firms see to it that their apprentices of all grades make full use of part-time day courses; at the B.A.C., for instance, practically all apprentices not only attend courses during working hours throughout their apprenticeship, but also sit for the appropriate examination each year. However, many employers take a short view of the value of technical education for any but the few brightest apprentices. The fact that the great majority of apprentices are now given day release for the attendance of technical courses is very largely due to the powerful pressure of the National Service Deferment Board. When National Service ends and the Board ceases to exist, it is therefore strongly desirable that this valuable function of the Board should be continued by another public body, pending the introduction of compulsory part-time education of all young workers.

Apprenticeship is, generally speaking, the only accredited form of training for industry in this country and it covers only a minority of young workers. But apprenticeship is not the only way of entering occupations that require skill: there are large industries with skilled workers but without apprenticeship; and in the industries with apprenticeship great numbers of dilutees and other semi-skilled operatives are now doing 'skilled men's work' or closely similar work.

Furthermore, the highly mechanised and intricately organised economic system of today has little use for the 'ox-like man'; in modern conditions the whole working population is required to be literate, machine-minded and adaptable. Training for industry of all young workers is of supreme importance for their own sake as well as for the sake of the country's productivity.

Therefore, besides the question of how all those within the apprenticeship system are to be adequately trained, there arises the second question of what part apprenticeship is to play in the training of that majority of young workers who are at present outside the apprenticeship system. Can apprenticeship be 'democratised', i.e. extended to provide training at all levels of requisite skill?

A few far-sighted and training-conscious firms pioneered in making their boy and girl labour attend day-continuation classes; and some others, public employers among them, have followed their example; in some works, too, there are initiation courses for all young operatives. The Central Youth Employment Executive has been endeavouring to spread such arrangements throughout industry, by promoting National Schemes for the Recruitment and Training of Young Persons for Industry. But the success of this policy has not been very great. Nor is this, on general grounds, surprising: it is of the essence of the present apprenticeship system to be exclusive because it is geared so as to serve vested interests; a training system of this stamp cannot be expected to be democratised. Such a state of affairs urgently calls for remedial action, for

CONCLUSIONS

'the educational system of a country can be, even more than its state organisation and its industrial organisation, its most valuable economic asset.'[1]

As a form of training, whatever its shortcomings, apprenticeship evidently makes a positive contribution to the country's productivity. But in its second role, that of forming the basis of a widespread system of restrictive practices, the apprenticeship system makes a negative contribution to productivity. Rigid demarcation between trades in particular impedes good manpower utilisation, thereby lowering the efficiency and increasing the cost of production.

Together with other matters related to the apprenticeship system, the practice of restriction has been adjusted to change. In Engineering, trade unions acknowledge de-skilling by the transformation of their structure (craft unions giving way to multi-grade unions) and by their apprenticeship policy: direct limitation of the number of apprentices has become an exception, and the unions' agreement to dilution does away with the claim to the recognition of apprenticeship as the only entry into a skilled trade. But while particular features are altered, the *gestalt* of the apprenticeship system is preserved: demarcation, formerly exclusive to apprenticed craftsmen, is now extended to a much wider class of workers, with further damage to productivity.

It may be objected that this aspect of apprenticeship is only incidental; that, purified from its association with craft particularism, apprenticeship could function with social benefit as a form of industrial training. The answer is that, as a historical fact, apprenticeship grew up as an integral part of a system of craft restrictionism,[2] and that it is today very closely associated with it. It may be possible to separate the educational

---

[1] H. D. Dickinson, *op. cit.*, p.58.

[2] The restrictive apprenticeship stipulations of the 1563 Statute of Artificers 'fitted also into the framework of the agrarian mercantilism which was the characteristic objective of government regulation in Tudor and Stuart England'. Margaret Gay Davies, *The Enforcement of English Apprenticeship* 1563-1642, p.257. Harvard U.P., 1956.

from the restrictive functions of apprenticeship; but this will be a difficult task.

To recapitulate, employers and trade unions have found a *modus vivendi* as regards apprenticeship which is a compromise of a sort but which reduces current productivity and trammels the flexibility of the economy. The main points on which the parties have given way to each other are these :—The trade unions have acquiesced in the scanty training given to great numbers of craft apprentices and in dilution, i.e. the up-grading, without formal training, of semi-skilled operatives. The employers have acquiesced in the continued recognition of de-skilled occupations as apprenticeable trades and thereby in the existence of a privileged group of workers, non-justified by superior skill; they have also by and large agreed to the rigid demarcation between the jobs not only of craftsmen but also of dilutees. In leaving the majority of workers, who are outside the apprenticeship system, without the training which is required in the national interest, the attitude of the two sides of industry is the same, for different reasons: the employers' reason is the costs of training; the craft unions' motive is that of maintaining exclusiveness of training as a means for protecting the privileges of their members. So long as the unnecessarily high costs of these arrangements can be passed on to the domestic consumer, and so long as the urgent need for competitive prices in the world markets is not brought home to industry, the two sides of industry are not likely to change their apprenticeship policy. The apprenticeship system with all its failings is sheltered by the full-employment policy and by the hingeing of wages on the costs of production via the cost-of-living index.[1]

The following denouncement by the Webbs is still applicable today, even though particular parts of the apprenticeship system have been modified; it is unfortunate that their anticipation of the consequent policy has so far not come true. 'Undemocratic in its scope, unscientific in its educational methods, and fundamentally unsound in its financial aspects,

---

[1] This is not intended as an attack upon these policies. It is intended to emphasise the view that such policies increase the need for radical reform of the apprenticeship system.

the apprenticeship system, in spite of all the practical arguments in its favour, is not likely to be deliberately revived by a modern democracy.'[1]

Recommendations for the development of training for industry must be based upon the inherent trends of apprentice training on the one hand, and on the other hand upon national desiderata.

The pertinent characteristics and trends are :—

The specific manual skill required for many crafts is reduced and narrowed; it can be acquired in a short period, especially by modern training methods; the tendency is for training to be separated from production.

Higher standards of literacy and general knowledge are required.

Technical education is becoming increasingly important for all grades of apprenticeship.

Reflection on the changes in content and method of training forces us to question whether works-based apprenticeship is still the right form of training today. The firms' co-operation in the training of workers remains necessary, to give them shopfloor experience. But the logical development would seem to be a reversal of the roles played by employers and technical colleges: full-time education, both practical and theoretical, at the college, with part-time release to works, perhaps in the manner of block-release. The duration of training would in most cases be much shorter than the present term of apprenticeship.

This proposition falls in with the conclusion which emerges from the difference between vested interests in apprenticeship and the national interest: in modern conditions, the individual firm should no longer have to bear the sole or even the chief responsibility for apprentice training. We would even go further and say that it does not seem advisable to put the decision on the numbers to be trained and the responsibility for apprentice training on industries or sections of industry. Our reasons, in addition to the foregoing argument, lie in the overlapping of industries and continual changes of the lines

[1] *Industrial Democracy,* p.481.

dividing them; the smallness and localisation of many sections of industry; the vicissitudes that may befall any of them, large or small; the employment of craftsmen of a given trade in many different industries (the main instance is that of engineers working in non-engineering industries).

As regards the trade unions, the national interest (including the long-term interest of the manual workers) would be best served if apprenticeship were divested entirely of the function of preserving obsolete and restrictive occupational barriers in industry, and became a social institution dealing solely with education and industrial training and extended to the whole working population. In spite of the appearance of adamant resistance to such a transfiguration of the apprenticeship system, there are developments in the trade-union movement today which hold out some hope for the emergence of an attitude more in line with modern conditions.

Considering all circumstances, the national interest would seem to require that the State must take the prime responsibility for training for industry, both in its quantitative and in its qualitative aspects.

INDEX

INDEX

INDEX

Education, liberal, 36, 137, 193 ; *see also* Literacy ; Skill, change ; Training non-apprentices

Ministry of, 18, 24, 36*n*, 137*n*. ; *see also* Further Education ; National Certificate

Educational gap, 34–5, 78, 117 ; level, modern-school leavers, 22, 64, 75 ; *see also* Technical courses, admission to ; opportunity, 15, 22, 133

Electrical Trades Union, 146, 173

Electrotypers and Stereotypers, National Society of, 5, 54, 72–3

E.M.I. Ltd., 88, 178

Employment Exchanges, 4, 41, 184–5 ; and Training Act, 1948, 40

Engineering, Apprenticeship in : ' Engineering apprenticeship ', term, 70, 88 ; Grading, 2, 32–3, 85–9 ; Indentures and National Scheme, 26, 28–9 ; Number of apprentices, 56–63 ; Probation, 77–8 ; Rural area, in, 177–82 *pass.*, Selection, 69–70 ; Size of firms, 57–63, 82, 90–5 *pass* ; Technical education, 37–40, 112–5, 119–37 ; Trade unions and, 148, 165–6 ; *see also* Amalg. Engineering Union ; Training conditions, 89–97

Engineering & Allied Employers' West of England Association, 4

Manufacturers' Association, Bristol, 4

Union, Amalgamated, *see* Amalgamated Engineering Union

'Equal rights clause' (Printing), 167

Evening classes, 36, 115–6, 118, 120, 123, 183

Evening Institutes, 36

Examination, *see* City & Guild certificates ; National Certificates results, 116, 128–31 ; *see also* Wastage

FEMALE workers, 44, 156, 181, 194

Firm, Size of, *see* under name of industries ; use of term, 5*n*.

Flanders, A., 150*n*.

Floud, J., 22*n*.

Foden, F. E., 132*n*.

Foremen, 5 ; Building, 103–5 ; Engineering, 63, 70, 91–6 *pass.*, 105 ; Printing, 100

Forward, 166*n*.

Foundry work, 70, 164, 182; unions, 164

Frisby, C. B., 111*n*.

Frustration of apprentices, *see* Interest in work

Full Employment, 10, 64, 157, 165, 190 policy, 152, 196

Further Education, *see* Technical Education; Office, Bristol, 4

Regional Council, 4

Statistical returns, 111, 125*n*.

GEORGE, J. C., 112*n*.

Germany, Western, 43*n*., 140

Government Grants, Technical education, 35–6, 114, 137, 182, 191

Training Allowances Scheme, 176 f.

Youth Employment Work, 41*n*., 184*n*.

Government Training Centre, 4, 8

Grading of apprenticeships, 32–3, 59–62 *pass.*, 85–9, 124, 191–2 ; *see also* National Certificate ; Technicians

Group Apprenticeship Schemes, 97–8

HALSEY, A. H., 22*n*.

Handyman, 181

Haslegrave, H. C., 92*n*.

Hilton, J., 7*n*., 161*n*.

Hogan, J. M., 22*n*.

IMPROVERS, 7–8

Ince Report, 40*n*., 176*n*.

Indentures, 13, 24–31 *pass.*, 78*n*., 141-2

Industrial Training Council, 15

Industries, order of discussion, 26*n*. ; sections of, 16, 24, 43, 197–8 ; without apprentices, 2, 3, 43, 145, 174–5

Inspectors of Schools, H.M., 4

Institution, Apprenticeship as a Social, 14–18, 173*n*., 174

Institutions of Electrical, Mechanical etc. Engineers, *see* Professional in, stitutions

Intelligence, Measured, 22

Interchangeable work, 161

Interest in work, 67–8, 75, 96–7, 192

INDEX

INDEX

For Product Safety Concerns and Information please contact our EU
representative GPSR@taylorandfrancis.com
Taylor & Francis Verlag GmbH, Kaufingerstraße 24, 80331 München, Germany